Man Who Could Work Miracles
A Critical Text

The Annotated H.G. Wells series
edited by Leon Stover and published by McFarland

Volume 1. *The Time Machine: An Invention.
A Critical Text of the 1895 London First Edition, with
an Introduction and Appendices* (1996; paperback 2012)

Volume 2. *The Island of Doctor Moreau. A Critical Text
of the 1896 London First Edition, with an Introduction
and Appendices* (1996; paperback 2012)

Volume 3. *The Invisible Man: A Grotesque Romance.
A Critical Text of the 1897 New York First Edition, with an
Introduction and Appendices* (1998; paperback 2012)

Volume 4. *The War of the Worlds. A Critical Text
of the 1898 London First Edition, with an Introduction,
Illustrations and Appendices* (2001; paperback 2012)

Volume 5. *When the Sleeper Wakes. A Critical Text of the
1899 New York and London First Edition, with an
Introduction and Appendices* (2000; paperback 2012)

Volume 6. *The First Men in the Moon. A Critical Text
of the 1901 London First Edition, with an Introduction
and Appendices* (1998; paperback 2012)

Volume 7. *The Sea Lady: A Tissue of Moonshine.
A Critical Text of the 1902 London First Edition, with an
Introduction and Appendices* (2001; paperback 2012)

Volume 8. *Man Who Could Work Miracles. A Critical Text
of the 1936 New York First Edition, with an Introduction
and Appendices* (2003; paperback 2012)

Volume 9. *Things to Come. A Critical Text of the 1935
London First Edition, with an Introduction and
Appendices* (2007; paperback 2012)

Man Who Could Work Miracles

A Critical Text of the 1936 New York First Edition, with an Introduction and Appendices

H. G. Wells

Edited by Leon Stover

THE ANNOTATED H.G. WELLS, 8

McFarland & Company, Inc., Publishers
Jefferson, North Carolina

> *The present work is a reprint of the library bound edition of* Man Who Could Work Miracles: A Critical Text of the 1936 New York First Edition, with an Introduction and Appendices, *first published in 2003 by McFarland.*

Facing the title page: Alexander Korda and H.G. Wells in Korda's office, 1935. Publicity photograph released by London Film Productions.

LIBRARY OF CONGRESS CATALOGUING-IN-PUBLICATION DATA

Wells, H.G. (Herbert George), 1866–1946.
    Man who could work miracles : a critical text of the 1936 New York first edition, with an introduction and appendices / H.G. Wells ; edited by Leon Stover.
       p.   cm. — (The annotated H.G. Wells ; 8)
    Screenplay.
    Includes bibliographical references and index.

    ISBN 978-0-7864-6876-8
    softcover : acid free paper ∞

    I. Stover, Leon E.   II. Man who could work miracles (Motion picture).   III. Series: Wells, H.G. (Herbert George), 1866–1946. Selections ; 8.
PN1997.M15   2012
791.43'72 — dc21   2002013825

© 2003 Leon Stover. All rights reserved

No part of this book may be reproduced or transmitted in any form or by any means, electronic or mechanical, including photocopying or recording, or by any information storage and retrieval system, without permission in writing from the publisher.

Manufactured in the United States of America

McFarland & Company, Inc., Publishers
  Box 611, Jefferson, North Carolina 28640
      www.mcfarlandpub.com

For
wife Takeko Kawai Stover
and
publisher Robert Franklin:
true wonder workers

Preface

Man Who Could Work Miracles (1936, henceforth *Miracles*) is a charming film story by H.G. Wells, a companion piece to *Things to Come* (1935, film production 1936), not so charming. The latter is deadly serious, the former ostensibly a comedy.

The challenge of *Miracles*, about which little or nothing is written in the critical literature, is to sort out serious Wellsian ideas from witty ironical comment. The 1936 text is profoundly ambiguous, from the hand of a master of ambiguity.

A video tape of the London Film production (1937) is available from Vintage Classics in a perfect state of restoration.

Leon Stover, Ph.D., Litt.D.
Professor of Anthropology Emeritus
Illinois Institute of Technology

Chicago, Summer 2002

Table of Contents

Preface	viii
Introduction	1
1. The Text	1
2. Cosmic Vision	2
3. Sex and Politics	3
4. The Common Man	4
Man Who Could Work Miracles (1936)	7
(Annotated text of the first New York edition)	8
Appendices	
I. "The Man Who Could Work Miracles,"	
by H.G. Wells (1898)	95
II. "A Vision of Judgment," by H.G. Wells (1899)	111
III. "Under the Knife," by H.G. Wells (1896)	117
IV. ["If I Were Dictator of the World"],	
by H. G. Wells (1931)	130
Bibliography	139
Index	141

Beware of false prophets.

— Matthew 7:15

Introduction

1. The Text

My copy text is the 1936 New York edition, published in London by the Cresset Press. It appeared just as the 1937 London Film production was readied for release.

The film, scenario and dialogue by H.G. Wells, is *The Man Who Could Work Miracles*. *Miracles*, the film story, has not the article "the." Its companion film *Things to Come* (1936) was also preceded a year before by a film story (1935) of the same title.

Both films were produced by Alexander Korda, director and founder of London Film productions. Korda was a firm believer in getting outstanding authors to script films for his company. And the greatest of these had to be H.G. Wells, who was given unprecedented control over two films, one after the other. Both of them were instant box office failures. But never mind: Korda had done his duty to literary greatness. At this distance it is now possible to see that Wells remained faithful to his visionary powers and perfected artistic craftsmanship. The two film stories are consistent with the masterful artistry of the Victorian scientific romances that established his place in *Weltliteratur*. By 1926, with the constitution of the BBC and growth of the film industry itself, Wells lost his once vast world readership. The man of letters has been eclipsed ever since.

Why the two film stories are companion pieces, for all their obvious differences, is hinted at in the Frame of *Miracles*. Three cosmic powers, seen against the starry heavens, frame the story. They are

1. the Observer
2. the Power Giver
---
3. the Indifference

These correspond with the Hindu trinity that Wells (1934, Appendix I in Stover 1987) explains as cosmic forces in human affairs.

1. Brahma — Creation
2. Siva — Destruction, force

---

3. Vishnu — Possession, sexual lust

The Hindu gods in turn correspond with Plato's tripartite order,

1. Perfect Guardians, teachers
2. Auxiliary Guardians, soldiers

---

3. Producers, desire

In *Things to Come*, the World Council of Direction seats two ranks of neoplatonic Guardians, under a philosopher king (Oswald Cabal), whose job it is to keep the selfish masses producing for the State, not for themselves and a free market economy.

The line drawn between the first two numbers and number 3 indicates hierarchical society, going back to the Bronze Age times, once distributed throughout the Indo-European cultural domain from India to Ireland. Plato remembers it in his Iron Age city state, and Wells industrializes it for his ideal World State.

2. Cosmic Vision

In his monumental bestseller *The Outline of History* (1920), Wells reads the past like tea leaves and divines the future. Always he sets historical events within the impersonal framework of geological time, as he traces human evolution from apelike origins to cave men, primitive tribes, through the early civilizations to the modern nation-states. Finally, in the last chapter, "The Next Stage of History," he prognosticates the coming of a unified world state. Yet still that is but the beginning. Thereafter, globalized humanity "will presently stand upon this earth as upon a footstool, and stretch out its realm amidst the stars."

In his essay "The Human Adventure," Wells visualizes a unified human consciousness, in and through and by which we each will learn "knowing oneself indeed to be a being greater than one's personal accidents, knowing oneself for Man on his planet, flying swiftly to unmeasured destinies through the starry stillnesses of space" (1914: 415).

This is of course a nebulous nothing, but it perfectly expresses Wells's omnipresent cosmic vision. Overt in his nonfiction, it is implicit in his equally didactic fiction. *Miracles* is no exception, as is evident in the Frame.

Sometimes the two modalities of writing are merged in one comprehensive work of fiction. A good example is *The World Set Free* (1914a), a stupendous novel of ideas that recounts man's entire evolutionary history to the accomplished world state. Its utopian world dictator lays down the golden Promethean rule, "There is no absolute limit to either knowledge or power" (278).

Miracles asserts the same, save that all power is given a man of no knowledge, the common man concentrated as a Boss. Power in the wrong hands, a mistake of the democratic ideal, must invariably lead to chaos. The mistake is corrected in *Things to Come*.

3. Sex and Politics

The basis for good statesmanship in Wells is that politics be more important than sex; if sex be more important than politics, given only either/or possibilities, then the god Vishnu of the Hindu trinity prevails in human affairs and chaos results. In that case humanity is doomed to extinction, no future for it. The choice is Wells's unearthly utopia or oblivion.

In *Miracles*, the title figure is one George McWhirter Fotheringay, a common man, a little man, dominated by Vishnu. Only when power is given him does he express the Vishnu-like lust in his heart. He assembles all the world's rulers and leaders in one great hall, built instantly at his command, and demands they "run it better." Once that matter is settled (it isn't, with cataclysmic results), he will turn his attention to his attractive ladies in waiting.

In *Things to Come*, the Boss of Everytown, Rudolph the Victorious, rules one of many ministates that have survived the universal smashup of World War II. He is another common man, chanced to take local power in the midst of civilization's ruination. He is motivated still to make war for the sake of gathering a harem of beautiful ladies, women attracted to power. Rudolph's like are "cleaned up" by the Airmen led by John Cabal. His Air Dictatorship leads on to a perfected world dictatorship under his grandson Oswald. They have the right stuff to belong to a Wellsian ruling elite.

The Airmen, or Airpersons, include women, on the ground that women should work *with* men and not be their sexual possessions. This idea goes back to old Plato's Guardians. Not that they were in the least celibate. The mixed Guardians made free with each other, but with no romantic entanglements. Least of all did they get married. Their children were cared for by the State with no knowledge of their parents, a condition for good citizenship.

Wells is no less hostile to family and marriage. He says that the monogamous family is the taproot of capitalist society. It is a "fellowship of two based on cohabitation and protected by jealousy" (1934a:465). From this "partisanship for wife and family against the common welfare" (1914:395) getting and keeping in everything else follows. "The fierce jealousy of men for women and women for men is the very heart of all our social jealousies" (1913:96).

In *Socialism and the Family* (1906) Wells addresses the question, Will socialism destroy the home? Yes, but it will be replaced by a State Family. "Socialism says boldly that the State is the Over-Parent, the Outer-Parent" (57). Plato again.

4. The Common Man

Wells is nothing if not rabidly antidemocratic. Democracy "is my King Charles's head" (1914b:x). He alludes to the beheading of Charles I by Oliver Cromwell's Puritan revolutionaries. Indeed, his program is called "the new Cromwellism" (1902:189). Another tag (from the same source) is the New Republic, after Plato's *Republic*. A characteristic title is *After Democracy: Forecasts of the World State* (1932). Another is *Democracy Under Revision* (1927), as revised by Wellsian statism.

In *Things to Come*, as explained by Wells himself, the Airmen are avatars of Brahma and Siva, the two gods of the Hindu trinity who bring knowledge (wisdom) and power (force) together in joint sovereignty over the selfish desires of Vishnu. The Airmen are "men of steel, men of knowledge, men of power" (1934:140).

In *Miracles*, Mr. Fotheringay is an avatar of Vishnu. He represents the mystique of people power in the democracies. But his ignorant actions, when unlimited power to work miracles is given him, only expose that mystique for what it is: the "incapacity of the common man towards public affairs" (1927:25).

Mr. Fotheringay shows his profound ignorance of basic science when he extends the day for the world's decision makers assembled before him to decide on his proposal. He commands the earth to stop rotating. Momentum sweeps everything off the face of the planet.

George McWhirter Fotheringay is a comic name for a comical little man. His last name alludes to Fotheringhay Castle in England, where Mary, Queen of Scots was imprisoned in 1586 and executed the following year (Kenyon 1994:142f). She had challenged the legitimate heir to the English throne. Mr. Fotheringay would have lost his life, with everybody else in the cataclysm, had he not made himself invulnerable from the start. He then commands the world be restored as it was before power came to him.

Wellsian lesson: the common man is no damn good: untrustworthy, unreliable, ignorant and foolishly selfish. Democracy is untenable.

H. G. Wells

Man Who Could Work Miracles

text of the first New York
edition, 1936, with annotations

MAN WHO COULD WORK MIRACLES

A Film by H. G. WELLS

Based on the short story entitled

THE MAN WHO COULD WORK MIRACLES

1936 — THE MACMILLAN COMPANY — NEW YORK

CONTENTS

Introductory Remarks [10]*

THE FILM

PART
I	The Elemental Powers	[13]
II	The Gift	[17]
III	The First Miracle	[18]
IV	Period of Realisation	[21]
V	Mr. Fotheringay Perplexed	[24]
VI	The Affair of Mr. Winch	[32]
VIa	Love Interlude	[36]
VII	Business Opportunity	[39]
VIII	High Finance	[44]
IX	The Transfiguration of Ada Price	[49]
X	Taking Advice	[53]
XI	The Pacification of Colonel Winstanley	[59]
XII	The Colonel Pleads	[64]
XIII	Man of Action	[69]
XIV	Doubts on the Eve of the Millennium	[71]
XV	Death Comes Into the Picture	[74]
XVI	The Soliloquy	[78]
XVII	The World of George McWhirter Fotheringay	[80]
XVIII	The Last Moment	[88]
XIX	The Mighty Powers Make Their Comments	[90]
XX	Da Capo	[92]

*[Publisher's note: page references are to the present annotated edition.]

Introductory Remarks

THIS is a film of imaginative comedy. It is framed in a Brief Prologue and Epilogue, which point to its larger intimations. George McWhirter Fotheringay is a definite personality, a concrete human being, and from beginning to end he remains *himself*. All the characters are highly individualised characters—not symbols. They have to be *acted*. We put the Frame about this story to guard ourselves against the invasion (which will be fatal) during production of any weakening "symbolism" in sets, make up, music, dialogue or any other detail of production. All that must be real, real as can be, "actual," matter-of-fact, up to the last phase of the world catastrophe. The Frame on the other hand has to be as "sublime" as music and camera can make it. The Frame could be stripped off and the film would still remain a coherent imaginative story, but the Frame is necessary to broaden out the reference and make *Man who could work Miracles* a proper companion piece to *Things to Come*.

Note that the "end" rests on Fotheringay and not on the Frame. Fotheringay is *it*. In contrast with *Things to Come* this is a star film.[1]

The Music

THERE should be a steady flow of sustaining music to this film, gay passing into the grotesque and rising to immense passages of stormy

---

1. The star in the 1937 film is Roland Young, who plays the part of Mr. Fotheringay with complete understanding. *Things to Come*, however, is indeed more symbolic. Although the 1936 film has its stellar actors, Raymond Massey as John Cabal and Ralph Richardson as the Boss, it remains a highly impersonal vision of what is and what is to come in future.

As the title page of *Miracles* indicates, the film story draws on a short story, "The Man Who Could Work Miracles" (1898). Likewise *Things to Come* draws on a massive novel, *The Shape of Things to Come* (1933).

sound. There should be characteristic motifs to sustain certain special threads of interest.

Fotheringay for instance ought to have a cheerful, trivial, tripping, catching air (with a lurking possibility of pathos). He could sometimes whistle this air between his teeth in moments of indecision. Linked with this there should be a distinct flourish for his miracles—petty and comic at first and later, as the miracles increase in importance, becoming charged with portent and menace.

Even when there are long rhetorical speeches the music should be keeping on with its quiet comment as if a goblin orchestra was watching and enjoying the drama, ready to stand up in excitement at the stormy parts.

The introduction should have a certain calm grandeur which becomes troubled by a sort of throbbing and ends abruptly in a loud silence when the finger descends upon Fotheringay.

Throbbing in the music has not yet been adequately exploited in the cinema to enhance an approaching climax. It ought to be tried here.

THE FILM

MAN WHO COULD WORK MIRACLES

Man Who Could Work Miracles

PART I

THE ELEMENTAL POWERS

GRANDIOSE music.

The starry sky is seen as it might be seen on a clear frosty night in the temperate zone. At first *the arrangement of stars is unfamiliar*. There are strange nebulæ and two very bright constellations of seven and eleven stars respectively. At first the stars stream slowly across the screen while the Riders ride. Then at the point indicated by the letter A the familiar constellations appear, but somewhat flattened, distorted and foreshortened. At the point indicated by letter B they fall into place exactly as they are known to us—Orion high in the heavens.

Across the stars two Riders become more and more distinct. They are beautiful, naked, male figures on horses. They are at first thinly luminous and then they become opaque. The stars shine brightly through them, then the two Riders become more opaque and definite, so as to blot out the stars behind them. They give the effect of being bronze rather than flesh and blood. Their voices are heard, but it is not quite clear which speaks. The First Rider is called here the Observer. The Second Rider is called the Indifference. A third great elemental is named the Player or the Giver of Power. These names do not appear on the screen. They are unimportant, and are used here for convenience only.

The OBSERVER: "Our brother the Giver of Power is yonder, playing with his planet." Points.

The INDIFFERENCE: "That queer small planet with the live things upon it?"

He looks under his hand to shade his eyes from a bright star cluster close above them.

The OBSERVER: "Let us see what he is doing."

Here is the point A.

The great shapes of the two Riders pass forward across the screen, their horses sink down out of sight so that the observer and the indifference become the semi-transparent half-length bodies of mounted men to the left and right of the central figure. They come to rest in semi-profile to the audience, looking at the central figure. This is a third great shadowy shape, also of heroic form and beauty. He sits in an attitude recalling Rodin's Thinker, brooding over something between his feet. (This is the point B.) Between his feet, at first infinitely small, is the solar system. It becomes larger and, as it does, the two other Riders pass by extension out of the screen and so become mere voices. But the player is still there, shadowy, but now almost opaque, and filling the screen so that only the solar system and a few near stars can be seen between and through his feet.

The INDIFFERENCE: "Cannot you leave those nasty little animals alone?"

The PLAYER shakes his head. "These men?"

The OBSERVER: "They are such silly little creatures. Swarming and crawling. Why has the Master permitted them?"

The PLAYER: "They are pitifully small and weak. But—I like them."

The INDIFFERENCE: "What is the good of them? Squash them."

The PLAYER, after a pause: "No, I like them."

The OBSERVER: "Nonsense. They are nasty. They are mean and cruel and stupid. They are vain and greedy. They crawl over each other and kill and devour each other."

The PLAYER: "They are just weak."

The INDIFFERENCE: "Happily."

The PLAYER: "If they were not weak they might not be so pitiful. But their lives are so short and their efforts so feeble...."[2]

---

2. A typical Wellsian *aperçu* for which he had a ready answer. If men are weak and therefore pitiful, in time they are destined to grow in power. Individual men are mortal, shortlived, but Man the zoological abstraction is immortal; his germ plasm (today's DNA) lives on in continuity. In time, as men learn to appreciate this scientific fact, they must gather the Will to act on it, to find their happiness by living in and through the species, and so achieve undying glory for their kind, an open-ended future amidst the stars when the sun burns and earth is no longer habitable.

The Giver of Power is also called the Player because he is actively engaged,

The OBSERVER: "If they had Power they would be no better."
The PLAYER: "I am going to try that—I am going to give them all the Power I can."
The OBSERVER: "Don't. You are the Power-giver. You can give Power beyond measure. What will happen if these greedy, silly, human scabs, who can only breed and scramble, spread out among our stars?"[3]
The PLAYER: "You will see."
The OBSERVER: "Are you going to give all of them Power?"
The Player nods and smiles with his head looking down on the earth.
The OBSERVER: "But *limitless* Power? Power to do *anything*?"
The PLAYER: "There is a limit to the Power I can give. So the Master has decreed.... There is a bit of gritty stuff at the heart of every individual, no Power can touch. The Soul—the Individuality—that ultimate mystery only the Master can control. Their Wills—such as they are—are Free. But all else—every position, every circumstance is mine...."

The solar system slowly expands so that the Player also passes beyond the scope of the screen and becomes merely a voice. The three voices come from above and right and left. The solar system now occupies the main part of the screen against a background of stars.

The OBSERVER: "Now we shall see what their Souls amount to!"
The PLAYER: "The Will of Man—released!"
The OBSERVER: "Worms rampant."
The INDIFFERENCE: "They will defile the stars."
The OBSERVER: "Don't give Power to all of them. That would be an explosion. Try one or two first. Try just one."
The PLAYER: "That might not work."
The OBSERVER: "Try just one—and see what there is in the human heart."
The INDIFFERENCE: "Yes. Try one. Someone commonplace. A fair sample. Let him be able to do—anything. Give him the Power to work miracles—without limit."

---

unlike the detached Observer and the Indifference, in the question of human Will. He is in fact the cosmic Giver of Will that in due course must strengthen the species and make possible remote and mighty ends for it. One possible utopian outcome is projected in *Men Like Gods* (1923), naked as the Frame's elementals. Shameless nudity is also featured in *A Modern Utopia* (1905).

3. Another Wellsian *aperçu*, again answerable. If men "breed" like animals, the Malthusian problem can be solved by means of birth control advocated by Wells. If men "scramble" in senseless competition, that can be resolved by state socialism. Then, when men do finally "spread out among our stars," they will be a wiser race, themselves men like gods.

The PLAYER musingly: "Why not? Then perhaps we might see."

The solar system has been coming nearer and growing larger. By this time the earth is recognisable, coming into the foreground of the picture. The three heads appear close together, looking gravely down on the planet.

The PLAYER: "Just any little fellow. They are all very much alike. I'll take one haphazard."

He puts out his finger slowly towards the earth.

The earth grows larger against the starry heavens. The hand with its projecting finger, overwhelmingly large, approaches the little earth.

PART II

THE GIFT

MUSIC ("the music of the spheres") has been going on very faintly as the voices speak. It becomes more audible as the latter sentences are spoken and now rises to, or rather degenerates into an anxious, disturbing, protesting air and ends abruptly—to suggest such a dismayed apprehensive silence as might precede the putting of a spark to a magazine.

Then a church clock strikes nine.

Under a starry sky, Dewhinton, a little English country town,[4] is seen, dimly lit with a few gas lamps, lit-windows, road signs, etc. The camera trucks up to, into and through this and comes to a stop outside a public house. The street is deserted except for Mr. George McWhirter Fotheringay, who approaches the inn in a leisurely manner. He is a commonplace, pale-faced young man, assistant in the general store. In the stillness a beam of blackness in the shape of a finger tip descends upon the bowler hat of Mr. Fotheringay. It is held for a moment, a beam of blackness with a pulsating flicker in its darkness, as though obscure currents of Power were flowing down it. Then it fades out. Mr. Fotheringay is not apparently affected by this, or aware of it in any way. He pauses before the door, adjusts his hat and stick, and enters. As he opens the door there is a warm swell of argumentative voices.

---

4. Dewhinton typifies the local patriotism of small English towns, whilst Everytown in *Things to Come* is a composite of the world's major urban centers, not just cosmopolitan London. All get smashed. In post-war Everytown, its local Patriot Chief, the Boss, reasserts the very same village provincialism that brought on the war. Mr. Fotheringay is no more sophisticated than the Boss when it comes to global politics, far short of the Wellsian dictatorship proposed in Appendix IV.

PART III

THE FIRST MIRACLE

THE Long Dragon Inn, Dewhinton. It is the sort of inn to be found near the centre of any English small town. The scene is the Bar Parlour. The chief light is a large paraffin lamp hanging by a hook from the ceiling.[5]

Mr. Fotheringay has established himself in a leaning attitude against the bar. Facing him is a sturdy individual, Mr. Toddy Beamish, a builder in a small way. Behind the bar, wiping out a glass, is the rather portly barmaid, Miss Maybridge. Mr. Cox, the landlord, is in shirt-sleeves and rather in the background. A cyclist sits at a table to the left nearly under the lamp, listening with an air of profound inattention to the discussion. An old man with a dog by a table to the right, is wagging his head slowly from side to side with a certain air of disapproval. Shots fairly close up to the speakers.

TODDY BEAMISH: "Well, Mr. Fotheringay, *you* may not believe in Miracles—but I do. Not to believe in Miracles, I say, strikes at the very roots of religion."

Old man assents.

MISS MAYBRIDGE: "Of course, Mr. Beamish, there's Miracles—*and* Miracles."

FOTHERINGAY: "Exactly, Miss Maybridge. Now let's get clear what a miracle is. Some people would argue the sun rising every day is a miracle."

TODDY BEAMISH: "Some of us do."

FOTHERINGAY: "Not what I call a miracle. A miracle I say is something *contrariwise* to the usual course of nature done by power of will—something what couldn't happen—not without being specially willed."

---

5. This is *not* the nineteenth century. Wells always complained that tradition-bound Britain was the most unprogressive of industrial nations. The United States and Germany had built national power grids from the start of electric illumination. Most parts of Britain still relied on gas and kerosene (paraffin) lamps, even candles.

TODDY BEAMISH: "So *you* say."
FOTHERINGAY: "Well, you have to 'ave a definition." (Appeals to cyclist.) "What do *you* say, sir?"
Cyclist starts, clears his throat and expresses assent.
Fotheringay appeals to landlord Cox.
COX: "I'm not *in* this."
TODDY BEAMISH: "Well, I agree. Contrariwise to the usual course of nature. 'Ave it so. And what about it?"
FOTHERINGAY, pursuing his argument: "For instance. Here would be a miracle. The lamp here in the natural course of nature couldn't burn like that upsy-down, could it, Mr. Beamish?"
TODDY BEAMISH: "*You* say it couldn't."
FOTHERINGAY: "And you? Wah!—you don't mean to say—No?"
TODDY BEAMISH: "No. Well, it couldn't."
FOTHERINGAY: "Very well. Then here comes someone, as it might be me, along here, and he stands as it might be here, and he says to this lamp, as I might do, collecting all my will—and I'm doing it, mind you—I'm playing fair: 'Turn upsy-down, I tell you, without breaking, and go on burning steady and—' Ooer!"
The lamp obeys.
Close up of Mr. Fotheringay's amazement. He keeps his hand held out. Mouth open.
Scene of general consternation. The cyclist, who is nearly under the lamp, realises the danger, ducks and darts away. Miss Maybridge, polishing a glass in happy unconsciousness, turns, sees the amazing thing and screams. MR. COX, open-mouthed says: "'Ere! What the 'ell?" The old man's dog gets up and barks. The old man's apprehension of the situation comes slowly.
Close up of Mr. Fotheringay in a profuse perspiration. "It's not possible," he gasps. "I can't keep it up—it's *got* to drop."
The lamp falls and smashes chimney and shade. But there is no fire. The container of the lamp is a metal one and the paraffin is not spilt. The bar is in darkness until Cox brings another lamp from an inner room.
COX, with dangerous calm: "And now, Mr. Fotheringay, will you be so good as to explain this silly trick—before I chuck you out."
The CYCLIST, much agitated: "Silliest thing I've ever seen done."
TODDY BEAMISH: "Whatever made you do it?"
COX: "Outside is the place for you. Outside the Long Dragon for good and all."
MISS MAYBRIDGE: "'E's got to pay for two bitters, Mr. Cox."
COX: "And he's going to pay for a lamp-shade and chimney."

The OLD MAN suddenly breaking into a shout: "'E did it with wires. I knowed a girl once who did things like that. A bad girl she was—my *Lord!* Wires he did it with."

MR. FOTHERINGAY, recovering the power of speech: "Look here, Mr. Cox, I don't know what happened to that confounded lamp—more than anyone. I didn't touch it. I *swear* I didn't touch it."

Close up of incredulous faces as Fotheringay sees them.

MR. COX, particularly implacable: "Look you here, Mr. Conjurer, don't let's have any more pother. You get out of my house before I shift you...."

PART IV

PERIOD OF REALISATION

THE vista of the village street lit not very brightly by gas lamps. MR. FOTHERINGAY, with his collar torn and his tie disarranged, is going home. He stops under a lamp. Close up of his face. "But what was it *'appened*? I don't understand what 'appened."

He continues on his way. Stops under another lamp. "Yes—but what *did* 'appen?" A man puzzled profoundly. His face under a third lamp. He makes movements of the hands to recall the movement of the lamp.

Scene shifts to Mr. Fotheringay's bedroom in his lodging. A small, cheap, lodging-house room lit by a candle. Mr. Fotheringay has taken off coat and waistcoat and is removing his collar and tie. "No need for Mr. Cox to get violent."

He inspects the state of the buttonhole of his collar and puts collar and tie very carefully over the small square shabby looking-glass. He sinks into profound thought. "*I* didn't want the confounded lamp to upset."

He begins to have inklings of how things are. His lips repeats arguments noiselessly.

"Miracles.... It was just when I said, 'Ere, you be turned upsy-down!'"

He starts with a sudden thought. He stares a prolonged stare at the candle beside him. He makes as if to speak and does not do so. He lifts a hand, half-pointing to the candle, and drops it irresolutely. He is evidently afraid of the possible success of the experiment he contemplates. At last he says, "'Ere. You be lifted up about a foot."

The burning candle is lifted up.

FOTHERINGAY: "Now—now—now—don't lose your head, George McWhirter Fotheringay, don't lose your head. It isn't going to drop if you don't let it down." Watches it almost appealingly. "No...."

FOTHERINGAY: "Now, keep burning steady, don't drop any nasty grease about or we shall get into trouble, and now over you go, upsy-down."

The burning candle obeys.

FOTHERINGAY's confirmatory grimace: he is beginning to realise his mastery. Almost casually he says: "As you were—on the table."

Candle behaves as directed.

FOTHERINGAY sits down amazed: "Gaw! It's a miracle! It's really a blooming miracle. Why? one might make any amount of money on the music 'alls[6] with a trick like this."

He meditates: "I suppose I could do it to almost anything. The table? 'Ere!"

He gesticulates and speaks inaudibly. The table is raised up.

FOTHERINGAY considers the things on it: "Too risky to turn it over. Go down again." It does so with a bump. "Now—the bed?"

He regards the bed doubtfully. "Biggish." Then with a gesture of "Here goes" he addresses himself to the bed. It is raised.

FOTHERINGAY: "Don't bump on the floor, mind. Down you go—*quietly*."

FOTHERINGAY meditates: "Raising things—by will power."

He goes to the looking-glass, sticks out his chin and glares. "Will power. 'Ipnotism and all that. Now I wonder...."

He raises himself a foot or so—is obviously rather frightened and comes down again.

"Wonder what else I might be able to do."

He fiddles with the extinguisher of the candlestick. "'Ere, get big. Be one of those cones what conjurers have. See."

If possible, the extinguisher must *grow* to a cone. If not, it must change to one in Fotheringay's hand.

FOTHERINGAY: "Now, let's get something." He puts it down on the table and turns up his sleeves conjurer fashion. "Hey presto!"

Nothing happens. He speaks louder: "Hey presto! Let there be a kitten under this." He lifts the cone with a gesture. He addresses an imaginary audience: "You see, Ladies and Gentlemen! A healthy young kitten!"

The kitten looks round and jumps off the table.

FOTHERINGAY: "'Ere, Pussy. Pussy!"

He pursues the kitten which darts under the bed. Fotheringay

---

6. Music halls (variety theaters) dominated popular entertainment in Britain in the latter half of the nineteenth century. They survived movies and television, in some places, well into the mid-twentieth century with the usual musical numbers, stage magicians, and other performing arts (Gascoigne 1993: 436).

scratches his cheek in consternation. "Can't let her go there. These kittens! If it makes a mess there'll be the devil to pay with Ma Wilkins! 'Ere, Pussy! Diddums." He bends down calling: "Pussy! Pussy!" and presently scrambles under the bed. His feet are seen kicking about. "Come 'ere, I say." Kitten is heard spitting. "Drat it! You little *beast*."

He emerges ruefully and kneels up, examining his bleeding hand which is scratched. "Rotten little pincushion!" Is struck by an idea. Goes on all fours. Points. "'Ere, you. Be changed into a pincushion. Ah—*got* you!" He draws out a cat-shaped pincushion from under the bed. He regards it curiously and then puts it back under the cone. "Presto vanish!"

FOTHERINGAY to the cone: "Now, you be an extinguisher again and we won't say any more about *that*. No."

FOTHERINGAY meditates, sucking his scratches. "Got to be careful."

A fresh idea. "'Ere, you scratches—be cured."

FOTHERINGAY: "Lor! I could go on doing miracles all night, I suppose."

Clock strikes eleven.

FOTHERINGAY: "Bed-time, George McWhirter—bed-time."

He sits down on his bed and begins to unlace a shoe.

FOTHERINGAY: "Most 'stonishing thing that ever happened to me."

A later shot of the bedroom with Mr. Fotheringay in bed. The candle has burnt down to the candlestick. The bed is littered with two or three small rabbits, bunches of flowers, a walking-stick, a number of watches, two china cats. He is eating a bunch of (miraculous) grapes rather suspiciously.

The village clock strikes two.

"Crimes! it's two o'clock in the morning and I shall be late for shop. What shall I do with all this litter? 'Ere, all I've got 'ere by magic, *vanish*." (They vanish.) "Gollys! I've burnt my candle to a stump. Old Mother Wilkins[7] won't half talk in the morning."

He blows at the guttering, flaring candle. It will not go out until at last he says: "Oh, *go* out."

Instant darkness except for the dim window. The bed creaks.

---

7. His landlady who serves him his breakfast egg in the morning. She will see her candle burnt down and no doubt demand payment.

PART V

MR. FOTHERINGAY PERPLEXED

ALARM clock ringing. Church clock strikes seven. Burlesque Dawn music.

Fotheringay waking up. Stretches. Rubs his eyes. Starts up into a sitting position.

"It was a dream."

Questions himself mutely. Scratches cheek.

Makes the characteristic gesture for a miracle. Lips move.

A small rabbit appears on the counterpane and is vanished again.

"Gollys! It's *true*."

Makes a resolution. "I won't do any more of it—not for a day. No. I'll think it over.... Won't do. Miracles coming off your fingers before you hardly know. *No*, Mr. George McWhirter Fotheringay, it's going to make no end of trouble for you—if you don't watch it."

Fotheringay at breakfast.

His breakfast egg is bad. Smells it and looks resentful. He changes it into another. Has two more. Perplexity. "She'll want to know how the shells came 'ere. Where can I put them? Lord, it's going to be difficult. *I* know! 'Ere, you two shells, be changed into house flies and be off with you.... Not a bad way that."

Church clock strikes eight. Mr. Fotheringay rouses himself to depart—still very thoughtful.

Exterior of the premises of Grigsby and Blott, General Drapers.[8] Bill

---

   8. Wells as a boy had served as a lowly assistant in just such a dry goods establishment. He novelized that experience in *The Wheels of Chance* (1896), projecting it onto a young man who had stayed in the business (see facing page). Wells got out of it to pursue his education, eventually at the Normal School of Science. He then went on to a lengthy literary career (*d.* 1946 at 80).

   A related novel about lower middle-class life, *Kipps* (1905a), is subtitled *The Story of a Simple Soul*. The common man lacks the right stuff for utopist leadership as in Marxian philosophy. Wells the same year in *A Modern Utopia* (1905) elaborated on his opposite idea.

The shop assistant in *The Wheels of Chance* (1896). That situation still obtained in the mid–1930s, when Mr. Fotheringay clerked for Grigsby and Blott.

Stoker is seen in the large window dressing it. He is a conspicuously good-looking young man rather on the florid side, much handsomer than Fotheringay. Ada Price, the costume young lady, stands in the doorway between the window space and the shop floor and is conversing (inaudibly) with him. She is tall and dark and wears the long figure-displaying dress of the Costume Room. Her manner is coquettish. Stoker bends down as if to say something intimate to her. Fotheringay appears in street outside. A start of jealousy. They become aware of him. Ada Price hastily assumes an expression of blameless dignity. Informal greetings. Fotheringay enters shop.

The Haberdashery Department. Miss Maggie Hooper, a blonde of rich sentimental possibilities, with large dreamy blue eyes, is wearing her arm in a sling. Her very much freckled junior, EFFIE BRICKMAN, asks: "How's the arm, Miss Hooper?"

"Not so painful so long as I keep it in the sling and don't use it. I wear the sling to remind me. Oh, I'm so hungry to-day—I wish it was lunch."

EFFIE: "I haven't the heart for lunch."

MISS HOOPER: "Feeling ill?"

EFFIE: "Feeling freckled—freckled all over. I've got two more. Powder's no use, Maggie. I'd be *all* powder. And *he's* nasty about it. Oh well, never mind—what can't be cured must be endured. Who's *this* sneaking round from the Manchester?"[9]

MISS HOOPER: "Good mind to give him the cold shoulder."

EFFIE: "Only you can't. *I* know."

MISS HOOPER: "Oh, I could. But I don't want to."

EFFIE: "Two's company and three's none. I'm off."

MISS HOOPER: "You needn't go."

EFFIE: "Only I will. See?"

As she disappears Mr. Fotheringay comes along behind the counter. It is against the rules for him to desert his department, but this is the slack time of the day before the afternoon customers come in.

MISS HOOPER: "You don't often come to the Haberdashery nowadays, Mr. Fotheringay. New attraction in the Costumes, I presume. Oh, we know all about it."

FOTHERINGAY, fatuous smirk: "I keep my heart in this department, Miss Hooper."

"Reely?"

---

9. Refers to the department of cotton goods manufactured in the preeminent English textile mills of Manchester.

"Reely, D'you know I've been wanting to talk to you all day. All the morning."

"Reely?"

"Serious. Maggie.... Something—something queer's happened to me. I can't make head or tail of it."

MISS HOOPER: "Not been left money or won a lottery ticket?"

Fotheringay shakes his head.

"Something queer? Not fallen in love?"

"That happened long ago—as well you know, Miss Hooper."[10]

"Reely?"

"Reely."

Archness on both sides.

"They say you had more than was good for you at the Long Dragon last night and upset a lamp. It can't be *that*?"

"Well, it *is* about that. In a way. You see it's odd. It's like this. If I say let a thing happen, *it happens*."

"Sort of prophesy?"

"No—sort of miracle."

"Oh, go—*on*."

"No, truth, Maggie; I'll prove it. Look 'ere."

Creates a bunch of violets and hands it to her.

"Of course, that's a trick, Mr. Fotheringay. One of your sleight of hand tricks. But they're lovely violets. They reely are. You didn't get this bunch for sixpence, I know. It's a good trick. They just seemed to jump out of nothing. But if only one *could* work miracles. Just think of what you could do."

"F'rinstance?"

"Heal the sick."

"I never thought of that. Leastway—I *did* heal some scratches."

"Here's my sprained arm. What wouldn't I give just to lift things and put them away—and not think of it."

FOTHERINGAY: "*Well*."

He touches her arm: "Be all right. Lift it."

The arm is tried. Incredulity at first. "Mr. Fotheringay, you're a healer! You've got the gift of healing."

FOTHERINGAY: "It ain't everything I've got."

"But the *good* you might do!"

---

10. Actually it is the beauty Ada Price that Mr. Fotheringay secretly lusts after. Miss Hooper he merely respects for the common-sensical advice she might offer him.

"I s'pose I might. P'raps I will."

Miss Hooper twists her arm about. There is no doubt about the miracle.

"Now, there's Effie there—heartbroken about her freckles. Her fellow hates freckles and she keeps on getting fresh ones. Well,—"

"I'll try."

MISS HOOPER: calls Effie, who appears. "D'you know Mr. Fotheringay has a charm for freckles? He has. Do, do it, Mr. Fotheringay."

FOTHERINGAY: "Let all the freckles go" (hastily adds) "and your complexion be perfect."

Change.

MISS HOOPER: "*Oh!* Where's a mirror?"

Mirror.

EFFIE: "It's marvellous. How he did it, I *don't* know."

FOTHERINGAY: "And *I* don't know."

Bell rings. "There's the second course for dinner."

Scene: the dining room of Messrs. Grigsby and Blott. The midday dinner in progress. Passing of plates down a long table, etc. Fotheringay is in a central position, next to him is Miss Maggie Hooper and next beyond Miss Ada Price. Bill Stoker sits with his back to audience. And sideways is Effie of the dazzling complexion. A junior apprentice and others. At the head of the table sits the Housekeeper.

FOTHERINGAY talks: "How it came to me, I don't know. I just say to a thing: you be so and so or you do so and so, and it seems to happen. Maybe it's will power. I never dreamt I had it in me until last night."

BILL STOKER: "When you broke the lamp in the Long Dragon. We've heard of that."

HOUSEKEEPER: "Well, don't you go breaking anything here, Mr. Fotheringay. No miracles in the house *or* the shop. Please. This is a drapery establishment—not a Home of Magic.

MISS HOOPER: "But he cured my sprain! And look at *her*."

Admiration of Effie, who turns her head graciously.

HOUSEKEEPER: "All the same, it isn't wise. Major Grigsby is always fussing about breakages as it is. What he'd say if we began to throw lamps about, I *don't* know.

FOTHERINGAY: "Of course, if I was sure I was always going to have the gift I'd go on the Halls—straight away. I've been thinking of that."

BILL STOKER: "I wouldn't."

ADA: "What would *you* do, Mr. Stoker?"

BILL STOKER: "I'd do better than that."

FOTHERINGAY: "How?"

BILL STOKER: "You tell rabbits to come and violets to come and complexions to come and all that. You're like the Spirit of Nature, Fotheringay. But all that's small beer. What's to prevent you saying: 'Here, let's have a thousand pounds in my pocket? Or for the matter of that, let's have twenty thousand in the bank. And a motor car say—and a big house'."

HOUSEKEEPER: "But is it honest to do things like that?"

FOTHERINGAY: "Maybe there's a limit. Of course, it would be pleasant-like to have that money in the bank. I'll think of that."

MISS HOOPER: "But don't forget your gift of healing."

BILL STOKER: "He could have a miraculous hospital. What's to prevent him? He could start miraculous hospitals all over the place. Just go and clean up everybody once a week. It needn't stand in the way of the other things. And how about a miraculous tip or so for the Derby? Lord, if *I* had it, I'd launch out. I wouldn't go on honouring Grigsby and Blott with my services much longer."

HOUSEKEEPER: "Fair doos, Mr. Stoker. You'd have to give your month's notice."

ADA, with ambition and wild surmise in her eyes. She is seeing Fotheringay in a new light. "The things you might do. You could be rich. You could do anything you liked. You could give presents right and left. Why! you might go into Society, Mr. Fotheringay. You might meet all the celebrated people. You might go to court and see the King!"

BILL STOKER: "Music halls, indeed!"

FOTHERINGAY: "I didn't mean to let all this out so soon. I tell you I'm a bit afraid of it. I don't mean to do anything very much yet."

MISS HOOPER, with a slight flavour of antagonism to Ada: "You listen to me, Mr. Fotheringay. Don't you do anything *rash*. You didn't ought to go about doing miracles just anyhow. You oughtn't to turn your gifts to selfish ends."

BILL STOKER: "Oooh! Here's Uplift."

MISS HOOPER: "Yes, I mean it, Mr. Stoker. This gift of miracles and healing is something very serious. You ought to have advice about it, Mr. Fotheringay."

HOUSEKEEPER: "That's plain sense. You ought to have advice."

FOTHERINGAY scratching his cheek: "I suppose I ought. I didn't think of that."

MISS HOOPER: "There's Mr. Maydig, the new Baptist minister."

HOUSEKEEPER: "No, Mr. Fotheringay ought to go to the Vicar."

BILL STOKER: "And a nice mess they'll make of it for you—either of them. Righteous old buffers without any imagination—leastways the Vicar is. And Maydig's just a spouter. You take my advice, Fotheringay, and do yourself well. Don't give your gift away to anybody."[11]

ADA: "There isn't a woman in the world who wouldn't love to have a man work miracles for her."

Fotheringay glances at her.

MISS HOOPER: "You take advice, Mr. Fotheringay."

HOUSEKEEPER: "Will you collect the plates, Jane. There's rhubarb and custard or bread and butter pudding. Miracles or no miracles, we've got to get on; we can't sit here and keep the shop waiting."

Scene: The Manchester Department in Messrs. Grigsby and Blott's establishment at the end of a busy day. Nothing has been tidied up. There is a stack of goods at one end of the counter in a very disorganised state and there is unrolled and unfolded material upon the counter in great confusion. Fotheringay leans against the fixtures in a profound meditation, picking his teeth.

Enter to him Major Grigsby, boss of Grigsby and Blott. Fotheringay starts to attention, so to speak.

GRIGSBY: "Come, come, Mr. Fotheringay. What's the matter with you to-day? Here we are five minutes from closing time and look at it—look at it. It's in a hay. You've got half an hour of tidying before you."

FOTHERINGAY: "Sorry, sir. I've had a little worry to-day. But I won't be long." Makes as if to roll up a bit of material and then is struck by a thought.

He makes his characteristic gesture and speaks almost inaudibly: "Apple-pie order."

In an instant rolls roll up, goods fold themselves, stacks of goods straighten up and everything leaps to its place.

Grigsby is amazed. He stands agape. He and Fotheringay confront each other. Fotheringay with his hands on the counter.

FOTHERINGAY to ease the pause: "I said it wouldn't take long, sir."

"No. It *hasn't* taken long. I couldn't follow you. Queer—but—. Very, very queer. You're quite sure, Mr. Fotheringay, that this sort of thing doesn't damage the goods?"

FOTHERINGAY: "Does 'em good, sir."

Grigsby walks slowly across the scene still very dazed. He turns and

---

11. In the event, Mr. Fotheringay, avatar of Vishnu after all, takes Bill Stoker's advice to serve self interest. He uses his power to gather a harem of beauties including Ada Price. The climactic catastrophe soon follows.

looks at Fotheringay, who affects to be staring out of the department. Grigsby looks away and then turns again. Mutual scrutiny of two perplexed men. Exit Grigsby sideways with his eyes on Fotheringay. Dissolve on Fotheringay scratching his cheek.

PART VI

THE AFFAIR OF MR. WINCH

EVENING. The Street. The Long Dragon in the distance. Passers-by. Fotheringay is taking the air after the day's work. He carries a walking-stick. He walks towards the Long Dragon twirling his stick. Becomes irresolute. The twirling of his stick reflects his doubts. Stops and stands still, swings round on one leg and goes off in another direction. No close-up of this. It is all shot at a distance of about 30 yards.

Late evening. Bright moonlight. A stile by the roadside. Fotheringay is discovered sitting upon the stile. His expression is exalted; his eyes very wide open. He is halfway between inspiration and idiocy.

FOTHERINGAY: "I can do anything. I can do practically anything. If I wanted to do anything to that old moon I could do it.[12] All the saints and the science that ever was; it's nothing to what I can do. Who's afraid, I tell you. Who's afraid?"

He whacks the stile with his stick and breaks it. "Gaw! I broke my stick and it cost seven-and-six at Christmas. My favourite stick."

FOTHERINGAY addresses his stick pityingly: "Ah, *did* they? But wait a bit, old fellow—wait a bit. How about Master's gift of healing. We'll put that all right and better. 'Ere, be—not a stick but a tree—a rose tree, a great big rose tree, right there on the footpath—all covered with lovely roses—and get your breath."

FOTHERINGAY: "Hullo, who's that coming along the road? Old Bobby Winch. This won't do. Go back, I tell you. Lord!"

The rose tree recedes rapidly and hits Winch, one of the local police force, who is just looking round a bit, violently. He has just come in sight down the road. For a time Winch is seen in a sort of Laocoön conflict with a much too floriferous and thorny and abundant crimson-rambler rose.

---

12. This hints at the Joshua-like miracle at note 43 where the sun appears to stop in the sky at Fotheringay's command. In the biblical text (Joshua 10:12) the moon stops at the same time.

FOTHERINGAY: "Gollys! Leave him alone! Come off it. Let that rose tree vanish."

The rose tree vanishes.

Winch advances upon Fotheringay, who slides down off his stile and confronts him. Winch's helmet is disarranged. His face is abundantly scratched and his expression formidable.

WINCH: "Hullo, Mister. What's the game? What's this throwing about of brambles, eh?"

FOTHERINGAY: "I wasn't throwing any brambles. Fact is—well, what I was doing was just a bit of a miracle like."

WINCH: "Ooohoo! It's you, Mr. Miracle Worker. It's you, is it? This is how you spend your nights, eh? Just practising another one, eh? Well, this time you've done one trick too many. You've got yourself into real trouble."

FOTHERINGAY: "I didn't mean that bush to hurt you, Mr. Winch. I really didn't."

WINCH: "Well, you did. You've assaulted the police in the execution of their duty. From all I hear you've been making yourself a public nuisance for some time. *Now* you've done it."

FOTHERINGAY: "Well—but. It's easy explained."

WINCH: "I'm glad of that because you'll have a fair chance to explain it to the Superintendent."

FOTHERINGAY: "But, Mr. Winch, you don't mean to say that you're going to take it seriously like that."

WINCH: "It isn't me takes it seriously; it's the Law."

FOTHERINGAY almost tearful: "What, run me in! Me—so respectable. You can't do it, Mr. Winch."

WINCH: "I'm doing it now. Come along."

FOTHERINGAY: "I won't come."

WINCH: "You will."

FOTHERINGAY: "Oh, go to Hades! Why, I—"

FOTHERINGAY stops aghast. The policeman has vanished.

"Here! Gollys! He's gone." Fotheringay's face is more like a pale moon than ever. Whispers: "He's gone ... gone ... to ... Hades!"

FOTHERINGAY: "If I bring him back he'll tell everyone...."

Dissolve to a desolate place under a lurid light among rocks. Thin wisps of vapour rise from the soil. A strange, half-animal vegetation maintains a precarious hold on the rocks. Two grave phantoms in togas pass across the scene, conversing profoundly. They are unsubstantial and nearly transparent. Constable Winch appears abruptly, legs wide apart and amazed.

"Where *am* I?" Pushes helmet back and scratches his head.

WINCH: "He's got me into some sort of pitfall. There's no end to his tricks. It's—warm here. Hullo!" Small lizard-like creature runs across the foreground. Something flaps across overhead, but only its shadow is seen on the rocks.

Winch is evidently becoming frightened, but he bears up bravely. He takes out his notebook. "I'd better make a note of some of this." Produces stump of a pencil. "The young constable should always make a careful note. Now what was the exact time?" Consults wrist watch. "Why, the paper's going brown. Hot on the boots too. Phew!"

Scene flashes back to Fotheringay standing in the empty moonlit road.

FOTHERINGAY: "Hades? That can't be a nice place. I can't send a chap to Hades like that. Wonder where my little old stick is. Oh—let my stick come back here now—no, not broken. And now what am I to do about Winch?"

FOTHERINGAY appeals to the night: "What am I to do about Winch?"

FOTHERINGAY: "He can't come back. I can't have him staying—there ... *I* know! San Francisco! That's half round the world—nearly. Let Mr. Winch, wherever he is, go immediately to San Francisco. And—"

Instantaneous flash to a busy street in San Francisco.

All this scene is to be bright and clear and rather small. It is to have something of the effect of a scene watched through field-glasses at some distance. No voices. The music is of horns and buzzers and shouts, but very small like the horns of fairyland. (N.B. Since it is 12.30 A.M. in Essex, it is 4.30 P.M. in San Francisco.)

Just at the climax of a traffic stop Mr. Winch, notebook and pencil in hand and helmet rather askew, appears abruptly. Traffic is released. Disorganisation of traffic by an unexpected obstacle. Marvellous escapes of Mr. Winch. His own movements are precipitate, ill-advised but singularly fortunate. Pursued by two San Francisco cops and an irritated crowd he reaches the side-walk. There he makes a valiant attempt to run for it, knocks over a Chinese laundryman, upsets an apple-basket, gets a little way up a ladder and is caught by a cop and is lost sight of in a great and growing crowd of spectators.

Return to Mr. Fotheringay walking slowly homeward.

"I got to have advice. I certainly got to have advice. What I ought to do about 'im ultimately I *don't* know. Extraordinary power it is. If I remember to send him back every two or three days like that, that ought to be all right. But it isn't only Winch. No. And there's all these other ideas I keep on having—all these different ideas. Some of the things I'm beginning to think of—they frighten me...."

"Yet I might do them. Try them anyhow."

"That about Ada."[13]

A smiling expression shows the onset of an agreeable reverie.

"Take the shine out of Mr. Billy Stoker."

---

13. He now dwells on his lust for Ada Price, thinking to *make* her love him against her wish. But changing the human heart is the one thing the Giver of Power says in Part I is beyond him to give.

PART VIa

LOVE INTERLUDE

THE same moonlit night. A lane between overhanging high hedges, beneath which everything is very dim, emerges upon a clearer space as it debouches on the road. Two dark forms are seen bending together as they come down the lane discreetly. Their movements suggest participated guilt. As they emerge into the moonlight they are seen to be Ada and Billy Stoker.

ADA: "Well now, Bill, you can't say I don't love you any more."

BILL: "You're a darling, Ada. A perfect darling. *My* darling."

ADA: "*Your* darling really?"

BILL: "Really." He takes her in his arms and kisses her.

ADA, with a deep sigh: "It's lovely. It's heaven. Being like this. And to think you was jealous, Bill, of that poor little Fotheringay!"

BILL: "Him and his miracles!"

ADA: "It must be awful late, Bill."

BILL: "Gollys! past the half hour. Time we was indoors. Door will be locked. Have to ring."

ADA: "We can't go back together, Bill. Everyone would talk."

BILL: "Yes." He considers the situation. "You go back to the front door. And I'll go round the back and shin up the waterpipe to the men's dormitory.[14] I've done it before. The window's never fastened. I'll go off—round the lane, the lane you know."

ADA: "Don't fall down."

BILL: "Not me."

ADA: "Give us a last kiss, Bill."

The picture dissolves while they are still kissing.

---

14. In drapery establishments, as Wells remembers them from his boyhood apprenticeship, all shop assistants and counter-jumpers lived upstairs, men in a men's dormitory, women in a women's. Below, Ada Price mentions that Mr. Fotheringay is fortunate to live outside; although as we see in Part V, he still takes his meals with all the rest at one common table.

Ada is seen walking demurely along the street towards the audience and towards the establishment of Messrs. Grigsby and Blott. At a street corner there enters from the left MR. FOTHERINGAY, deep in a lover's meditation.

"Why, Ada! The very girl I was thinking of!"

ADA: "Why, it's George! D'you know the time, George? It's nice to be you and live out and not have to be in by half past ten every night."

FOTHERINGAY, stopping before her: "I could stay out all night in moonlight like this, Ada. Couldn't you?"

ADA: "It's lovely. Yes, it's real lovely. Done any more miracles, George?"

FOTHERINGAY: "Well—nothing to speak of. Not much fun doing miracles alone. One wants an inspiration. F'r instance. Here—. See the church clock?"

They both look round. The church clock is seen showing a quarter to eleven.

FOTHERINGAY's voice: "Here, you—and every clock and watch in Dewhinton, go back twenty minutes—twenty-five minutes—*now*!"

The clock goes back.

Return to the street.

FOTHERINGAY is seen showing his wrist-watch to Ada by the light of a match. "See? My watch too! You're all right, Ada. If you have to ring and be let in, the hall clock will bear you out."

ADA: "That's what I call a Real Miracle, George. And a very nice one."

FOTHERINGAY: "It's nothing to what I *could* do—for *you*, Ada. D'you know why I made it twenty-five minutes instead of twenty? Just to have a bit of a word with *you*, Ada. See?"

A coquettish: "Well, you *deserve* five minutes, George."

FOTHERINGAY: "I deserve a lot more than that. I'd do—oh, I'd do extraordinary things for you, Ada. You seem to stir up my imagination."

ADA: "It's very kind what you *have* done."

FOTHERINGAY: "Oh, Ada. I'd do anything—if I could get you to sort of love me. Indeed I would. If I could get you—so's you wanted to kiss me."

ADA: "Oh, George! Miracles or no miracles, you mustn't talk to me like that."

FOTHERINGAY: "Why shouldn't I? Don't you care for me? Not a little bit?"

ADA: "Not in *that* way. No..." (She deliberately drops the George.) "Mr. Fotheringay."

FOTHERINGAY: "Why not?"

ADA: "I don't know. I just don't."

FOTHERINGAY: "Anyone else, Ada? Eh? *I* know."[15]

ADA: "That's not your business, Mr. Fotheringay. Anyhow, I don't care for you like that. Not in that way. You're a nice chap but not *my* sort of chap. It isn't your fault, or my fault, or anybody's fault. If there is anyone or no one it wouldn't make any difference about us. I couldn't love you."

FOTHERINGAY: "No?"

ADA: "No. And that's that."

FOTHERINGAY: "Here, wait a bit, Ada! Hold on! Are you so sure you're never going to love me? How about a miracle? How about making you?"

ADA: "You couldn't do that, Mr. Fotheringay." (Frightened, she recoils.) "You *wouldn't* do that, Mr. Fotheringay."

FOTHERINGAY: "Oh! Now, let me see, my lady. Let's see what we can do. *Won't* I do it! Here, now—you be in love with me. You be hopelessly in love with me now. Forget all about Bill Stoker and be in love with me. *Now.*"

She stares at him fascinated. For a moment she says nothing. Then she whispers: "*No.*" (Then, louder.) "No." (Then aloud, exultantly.) "*No*. No, I'm not a bit more in love with you than I was. It doesn't work. It doesn't work, Mr. Fotheringay. No, I'm not changed a bit about you. You and your tricks. I'm not an old clock or a rabbit or anything like that. But you frightened me, Mr. Fotheringay. Oh! You *did* frighten me." She looks at him, still a bit afraid. "Time I was in, Mr. Fotheringay." She turns and runs off. "Goodnight."

---

15. It is of course Bill Stoker. Not only is Mr. Fotheringay lustful, he is also sexually jealous, another attribute of Vishnu the Possessor, the common man's divinity. For all the high-minded advice he gets from the Reverend Maydig in Part X, Mr. Fotheringay instinctively rejects it, and in the end naturally follows Stoker's advice to be selfish with his gift.

PART VII

BUSINESS OPPORTUNITY

MAJOR Grigsby in his inner sanctum in the establishment of Grigsby and Blott. The Major is a self-important, shortish man of the military shop-walker type. His sanctum is separated by a glass partition from the counting-house beyond which is a glimpse of the general shop. Papers and patterns and one lady's hat on a stand adorn the large desk at which the Major is sitting. The Major is thinking out what he has to say to Fotheringay. He rehearses phrases in dumb show. Finally touches a bell on his desk. Small boy apprentice appears. "Send Fotheringay to me. No—no. Ask Mr. Fotheringay to come to see me."

Rehearses more than ever. Gets up and walks up and down the little office—in silent argument.

FOTHERINGAY appears, or at least his forehead and nose appear, above the frosted part of the glass pane of the door of the sanctum. Habit makes him defer to Grigsby but there is a growing self-confidence in his manner. He surveys the Major and the Major surveys him. He opens the door slowly and says with a politeness that is not in the least abject: "You wished to see me, sir?"

Grigsby, in true shop-walker fashion, places the second office-chair for him. Then, recalling their respective stations, he walks round his desk.

GRIGSBY takes his seat at the desk: "Sit down, Mr. Fotheringay, I want to talk with you." Fotheringay takes the other chair.

Grigsby at his desk becomes the great business organiser; the man of penetration and character. Fotheringay is, as usual, uncertain about himself, distracted between his new sense of power and his old sense of inferiority. He is typically the human being with a gift.

GRIGSBY: "Well, yes. I want a talk with you. Fact is—Mr. Fotheringay, I couldn't help being struck by the way you tidied up your department last night. Very much struck. Practically instantaneous. Could you—ah—could you" (Head on one side) "—tell me in any way how you managed it? I'm told it isn't the only thing of that sort you have done."

FOTHERINGAY is vaguely on his guard—he hardly knows against

what. "I could tell you—and, so to speak, I couldn't. I suppose, roughly, it's what one might call a miracle."

GRIGSBY: "Isn't that rather an old-fashioned word, Miracle?"

FOTHERINGAY: "Well, suppose one said it was something—something contrariwise to the course of nature done by an act of will."

GRIGSBY: "Ah, *will*. Now there is something I can understand. A man doesn't build up a big and vital business like this—with three branches already and forty-nine assistants—out of one small shop with five hands, in seven short years, without knowing something of Will Power. Will Power over assistants, over partners, over customers.... But frankly, Mr. Fotheringay, you haven't struck me as the kind of young man who went in for that sort of thing."

FOTHERINGAY: "I haven't. It's just come to me."

GRIGSBY: "You never studied Dominance—never exercised your will against other wills?"

FOTHERINGAY: "Only occasionally, I suppose, with customers."

GRIGSBY: "And that not very successfully."

FOTHERINGAY: "Even now I don't seem able to do much with that. It's miracles—well, just old-fashioned miracles I do—like magic, bit of healing and that style of stuff, making things and animals appear and disappear; moving things and people about like from here to there. Changing things. That it seems I can do practically without limit. I never knew it before—but I can."

GRIGSBY beginning to concentrate on him and pointing a compelling finger: "But not to get down to feelings and motives?"

FOTHERINGAY: "No, I don't seem able to do that."

GRIGSBY: "Have you tried?"

FOTHERINGAY evasively: "It wasn't much good."

GRIGSBY: "But tell me—tell me."

FOTHERINGAY: "It was only that I wanted someone to feel differently about me. It wasn't anything. Never mind about that."

GRIGSBY: "Lady in the case? Well, we won't talk about that. Nothing in that direction—no. Coming down to solid fact, Mr. Fotheringay, I want to make you a business proposition. Now. Now—. I take it that even if you can't absolutely *make* 'em want to come in and buy, you can offer inducements—considerable inducements. Efficiency. Service. F'r instance, you could straighten up our shops, open them in the morning, deliver our parcels to the addresses given... All by miracle, eh? Have you thought of that, eh? Why not? I've been thinking of the way you straightened up that department last night. I do that at times. Think things out in the small hours. My mental life—few people suspect it. *Intense* concentration. Now, here we are! Grigsby, Blott and

Fotheringay, the Miracle Drapers. Naturally you contract to confine your gift entirely to our organisation. No outside miracles. Do you get me, Mr. Fotheringay?"

FOTHERINGAY: "Yes, but—"

GRIGSBY: "I've figured it out. I've figured it out in my head. We could guarantee you, sir, an income of £3,000 in the first year—three thousand pounds! There isn't a competitor we couldn't down by sheer rapidity and economy. We could extend over the west coast, over England. There's no limit with an advantage like that. Call me a dreamer, Mr. Fotheringay. I tell you every great business organiser is a dreamer. The Poetry of Commerce! But I can see Grigsby, Blott and Fotheringay now, from this chair, running into millions of capital and spreading all round the world."

FOTHERINGAY: "All round the world, eh?"

GRIGSBY: "All round the world!"[16]

FOTHERINGAY, deep in thought for a moment. "I suppose, sir, San Francisco *is* pretty near all round the world, isn't it?"

GRIGSBY: "Practically so—essentially so. Why?"

FOTHERINGAY: "Thought struck me. I suppose you don't know, sir, how long it takes to get here from San Francisco?"

GRIGSBY: "Three weeks or a month I should think. Why do you ask?"

FOTHERINGAY: "Three weeks anyhow?"

GRIGSBY: "*All* that. Why do you ask?"

FOTHERINGAY: "I just wanted to know. I've got a sort of relation there."

Flash to a brief bright scene in a San Francisco hospital. Mr. Winch's clothes, belt and helmet are seen hanging on a peg or in a cupboard, and being scrutinised by the typical gangster reporter (Y) of the films. To him comes another more intelligent type (X below). (The reporters who speak are X, Y, Z.) The picture comes round to Mr. Winch with a bandaged head sitting in a wheeled chair surrounded by baffled (typical) newspaper-men.

X: "And that's all you've got to tell us, Mr. Winch?"

---

16. Grigsby is not a false "dreamer." At bottom he appreciates the Wellsian idea of a global economy. The fact that he titles himself "Major," a military rank no doubt gained in World War I, should not detract. Nor should his monopolistic insistence above that Mr. Fotheringay confine his gift to the firm for the sake of private-profit capitalism. What seems to be the author's ironic commentary has his own real grit concealed within it.

WINCH: "That's all I got to tell you."

Y: "Wal—it's Crazy."

Z: "It don't *begin* to make sense."

Winch goes out of the picture which comes to a conversational close-up of the reporters. There is one man, X, with a finer mind than the others and he is most impressed by the whole affair.

Y: "You can't make a story of that, boys—he's screwy."

Z: "What's all the dope about roses and brambles—anyhow?"

X: "These clothes he's got are the real genuine English cop's uniform. I tell you there's something in it. Fourth Dimension, or something."

Y: "Where'd he scram from? That's the only thing in it that interests *me*."

X: "How about the clothes?"

Z: "Aw, to hell with the clothes! The Ed won't print a line of the stuff. We can have people *disappearing* all over the United States. That's fair copy; that is. But this chap suddenly *appearing*. You can't stuff 'em with that."

X: "There's his clothes I tell you—and his poor little toasted notebook."

Z: "And notes you can't read!"

X: "But it's true. He's a genuine English cop and he's come straight from Essex here. In a flash. *How?* Lord knows. But he came so fast, his shoes and his book were frizzled."

Y: "Might make it a case of materialisation."

Z: "You try that on the mugs who read your sheet. I wanna keep my job."

Y: "Yes—kid 'em with it."

X: "This news racket is plain nuts. We're supposed to be always looking for something new. Well, here's something new—something that's never happened before. And because we can't fit it in on any of the stock stories—we've got to cut it out. We've got to cut it out, boys. Just as we should have had to cut out a story about flying or submarines or radio—fifty years ago. It's *new news* and the truth is you mustn't have new news in a newspaper. Wod! Wod! Of all the mean and feeble things that ever crawled on its belly in the mud, the human imagination is the meanest and feeblest! Here's the most wonderful and unaccountable thing that has ever happened—and we can't spill it...."

X reflects indignantly: "I'll make the front page with this yarn—or pass out. I'll bring imagination to bear on it somehow." Protesting face comes close up. "Can't they tell the Wonderful when they see it?[17] Are they *never* to be taken out of their mean little selves?"

Dissolve back to Major Grigsby talking to Fotheringay, who is not so much excited and convinced as being dragged along by the Major's compelling flow.

GRIGSBY: "You must bring imagination to bear on this. If you let this gift of yours just splash about—you'll waste it. It will do no good to you or anyone. Miracle here. Miracle there. Just scattering miracles. Cheap as dirt. But canalised—concentrated! Monopolised! Limited strictly to the expansion of Grigsby, Blott and Fotheringay, this can be an immsense thing!"

FOTHERINGAY: "All this is very *attractive*."

GRIGSBY: "Attractive. It's the logic of the situation. I see us springing up in a night to be giants in the distributing world—big business—big money—big men. Monopolists.[18] We can't miss it. I tell you what, Mr. Fotheringay. I'd like to have the reactions of Mr. Bampfylde to this— Mr. Bampfylde of the bank over the way."

---

17. Reporter X has got the Wellsian message just right. In *The Invisible Man*, one of scientific romances, the title figure reveals himself to the incredulous locals of the village inn to which he has retreated, and says, "You don't understand who I am or what I am" (see text at page 71 *n*78 in Stover 1996–2001, vol. 3). I annotated that remark by citing these words: "If a thing is sufficiently strange and great no one will perceive it. Men will go on in their own ways though one rose from the dead to tell them that the Kingdom of Heaven was at hand, though the Kingdom itself and all its glory became visible, blinding their eyes" (1915:313). This agrees with reporter X.

18. Again the Grigsby stress on monopoly (see note 16), as if that were the great evil under attack by socialists. But Wells, himself a professed socialist, proposed for his world state nothing less than a total government monopoly of the world's economy. It would run all business affairs better than profit-seeking businessmen, using their own methods on a global scale.

PART VIII

HIGH FINANCE

FOTHERINGAY, Major Grigsby and Mr. Bampfylde are discovered in a little parlour of the Dewhinton branch of the London and Essex Bank.

Mr. Bampfylde is a small, lean, dry, very "efficient" man, wearing a pince-nez. Grigsby is flushed and dishevelled with his own eloquence in propounding his new and wonderful scheme. Fotheringay seems to have done some thinking while the other two have been talking. By degrees the deference of conscious inferiority is evaporating from his manner. A certain native shrewdness and simplicity is becoming more apparent. And he is beginning to conceive of himself as a potential capitalist of importance. His attitude is easier. He does not "sit-up" as he did in Grigsby's sanctum.

BAMPFYLDE: "It's a most extraordinary proposition, Major Grigsby. If you had told me two hours ago that miracles would be worked in this parlour—and that I should be confronted with a project for a world net of miraculous chain stores[19] I should have scouted the idea—scouted the idea."

---

19. Bampfylde the investment banker enlarges on Grigsby's proposal with a bigger idea, one that will develop the existing trend toward the growth of department stores, in which dry goods are but one item. That is what he means by his emphasis on "a world net of miraculous chain stores," exactly what has come to be. Local retail shops have indeed become largely displaced by huge department stores, a worldwide transformation that is just as important as the other near-miraculous inventions of the twentieth century.

Wells did not fail to see it coming, and to sense utopian prospects. In his big treatise on social economies, *The Work, Wealth, and Happiness of Mankind* (1931), he glorifies the department store, "the concentrated giant store with an immense radius of delivery, to which people go for clothing, furnishings, provisions, *et cetera*" (246f). "This is 'mass distribution' to balance mass production" (254). Better, this hints at the socialist prospect of "ultra-modern State Capitalism" (557).

Why the socialist tag for this? Because Wells embraced a pre–Marxist

GRIGSBY: "And you don't now?"
BAMPFYLDE: "I do not."
GRIGSBY: "It took me a painful night to grasp all this. And get it in order."
BAMPFYLDE: "I shall have trouble with headquarters, but I think I can handle that. Mr. Fotheringay, I think you may count on having the London and Essex Bank behind you. I think you may count on us, Major Grigsby."
FOTHERINGAY: "Ye-es. I suppose this is how it ought to be done. I don't know much about finance and business management myself. But now—what you propose is that I be sort of exclusive."
GRIGSBY: "Confine your gift entirely to Grigsby, Blott and Fotheringay. That's—*essential*."
Bampfylde nods endorsement.
FOTHERINGAY: "It's just there I don't *see* it."
Both await his further utterance.
FOTHERINGAY: "Now there's the gift of healing—and that sort of thing. I don't want to make a business of that."
GRIGSBY, brilliant idea: "We could have free clinics in all our stores. Healing, Tuesdays and Fridays—and special bargain lines. Free. Absolutely without charge."
FOTHERINGAY: "Ye-es. We *might* do that. But what I don't see is—why don't we give away all the stuff free? Why make a business of it?"
GRIGSBY: "You can't do that. You positively can't do that."
FOTHERINGAY, yielding: "I suppose you can't. No. And then, why do we have to borrow money for it and—what did you call it?—issue debentures?"
BAMPFYLDE: "You must have the thing put on a sound financial basis."
FOTHERINGAY, trying to grasp it: "We got to make money by it."
GRIGSBY with profundity: "Solvency, sir, is the test of service."

---

school of socialism that was not communalistic but statist. He advocated "autocratic state capitalism" (1931a:63), the marriage of big business and government under State management. This idea had its actualization under the two fascist dictatorships of Mussolini's Italy and Hitler's Germany. It first obtained, from 1917, in the Soviet Union under the dictatorships of Lenin and then Stalin, save that all private property was confiscated by the State and managed directly by it. Wells approved, although he objected to a Marxist cover story for unadulterated state capitalism (see note 27). The State has to be the ultimate monopolist of monopolies, as in his world state.

FOTHERINGAY: "But why, if we want money, why not make money right away?"

BAMPFYLDE: "It can't be done." (Pause. Growing alarmed.) "Without quite disastrous results."

FOTHERINGAY: "But look here." (Holds out his hand and his lips move. A hundred pound note appears.)

BAMPFYLDE: "No. No! You can't do that. That's illegal. That's forgery. That note's a forged note."

FOTHERINGAY: "Look at it. All right, isn't it?"

BAMPFYLDE, fingering the note: "Oh, this won't do." (Gets up in his agitation.) "This will NOT do. You musn't make money when you want it. Strikes at the root of—everything. Puts the whole banking system out of gear. People must *want* money."

GRIGSBY: "And they've got to *want* commodities."[20]

FOTHERINGAY: "But if I can give them all they want!"

GRIGSBY and BAMPFYLDE together: "What would they DO? What incentive would there be for anybody—to do anything?"

FOTHERINGAY, scratching his cheek: "Couldn't they have some fun—like?"

GRIGSBY jumps up. Fotheringay sits perplexed but not protesting actively.

BAMPFYLDE: "I can assure you, Mr. Fotheringay—I can assure you. I have studied these questions—very profound questions—before you were born. Human society, I repeat, is based on want. Life is based on want. Wild-eyed visionaries—I name no names—may dream of a world without need. Cloud-cuckoo-land. It can't be done."

FOTHERINGAY: "It 'asn't been tried, 'as it?"

BAMPFYLDE: "It couldn't be tried."

FOTHERINGAY's face remains sceptical.

GRIGSBY: "You take my word for it, Mr. Fotheringay. You can't go just *heaping* things on people without a *quid pro quo*. It would ruin everything. Universal bankruptcy. Lassitude. Degeneration. Now, if only you will follow us—trust us… We have worked out this scheme for—

---

20. Again these seem like ironical comments. But in "Has the Money-Credit System a Mind?" for *The Banker* (1928), then finance capital's chief organ, Wells argues that investment banking is the life blood of an increasingly globalized economy. The only problem is, the money-credit system has not yet a controlling world brain. That in time will emerge, with his world state. Mr. Fotheringay is indeed foolish, contrariwise to nature, to create money out of thin air.

keeping your gift—your very dangerous gift, if I may say so—within bounds. Incidentally *you* will become a multi-millionaire. Not a doubt of it. And people will get what they want—within measure."

BAMPFYLDE: "A general encouraging gradual rise in prosperity. Nothing extravagant. Above all, no violent changes."

FOTHERINGAY: "I got to think it all over."

A shop vista in the establishment of Grigsby and Blott. At the far end the front door and street outside. An assistant serves a customer in the background. Close up. Bill Stoker is floor-walking in the absence of Major Grigsby. He adjusts a display of sunshades. Another assistant stands at the counter.

ASSISTANT: "Where's Fotheringay to-day?"

STOKER: "Haven't seen him all the morning. Governor sent for him."

ASSISTANT: "He's got the swap perhaps."

STOKER: "Likely enough."

ASSISTANT: "All this foolery with miracles!"

STOKER: "Only get him into trouble. *He* can't do anything with it. He's got no imagination. Now if only *I* could snatch it from him." (Twirls a sunshade and kisses his hand.)

Fotheringay appears from street in doorway down vista and advances up shop. A few days ago he would have been deferential to the customer and he would have dodged round behind the counter at once. Now he disregards the customer and marches in a brown study up the middle of the shop. He has a new air of responsibility about him. He looks up as he approaches Bill Stoker, regards him absent-mindedly and then nods.

STOKER: "Hullo Fotheringay, what's up? Where you been all the morning?"

ASSISTANT: "He's got the swap."

FOTHERINGAY shakes his head slowly—smiling slightly. He is fairly self-important but rather anxious to get their reactions to what he has to say. "Not it. I've been considering a business proposition. What do you think of Grigsby, Blott and Fotheringay, Miraculous Stores?"

ASSISTANT: "Oh! Get *out*!"

FOTHERINGAY: "Yes, I got a firm proposal. Big business. I didn't realise it before, but there's a lot of money in these miracles—properly handled. Big money."

STOKER: "Gee! Miraculous stores, eh?"

FOTHERINGAY: "That's about it."

ASSISTANT: "Put us all out of work."

FOTHERINGAY: "Didn't think of that."

STOKER: "You haven't signed on?"

FOTHERINGAY: "No. I sort of feel I ought to think it over."

STOKER: "Who's in it?"

FOTHERINGAY: "Oh, Grigsby—and the Bank."

STOKER: "Yes, but why make money for them? Why not make it for yourself?"

FOTHERINGAY: "I'd make money all right."

STOKER: "Why make it for *them?*" If you want money—make it for yourself. Why fatten up old Grigsby and Bampfylde?"

FOTHERINGAY: "You can't do it that way. You can't make money for yourself."

STOKER: "Why not?"

FOTHERINGAY: "Oh! Mr. Bampfylde has explained. He made it very clear. Lead to social chaos. Universal bankruptcy. Break up the social system."

STOKER: "Break up old Grigsby and Blott, you mean."

FOTHERINGAY: "He didn't think it ought to be done."

STOKER: "He'd do it fast enough if he knew how to do it himself. I tell you, Fotheringay, these chaps are just sucking on to you. Gaw, if *I* had your gift—"

FOTHERINGAY: "Well?"

STOKER: "I'd run the world."

Fotheringay looks at him with his head on one side.

STOKER: "What price Bill Stoker's New Deal? I'd make a world of it! I wouldn't put my gift into blinkers and harness it to Grigsby, Blott and Co. No fear!"

Fotheringay's face taking it in. It is a new but assimilable idea.

PART IX

THE TRANSFIGURATION OF ADA PRICE

THE costume department of Grigsby, Blott and Co. Dress stands with costumes. Mirrors. It is slack time and no customers are present. Miss Ada Price is discovered at a mirror, with her lipstick.

Fotheringay enters and stands regarding her. Mutual hesitation because of the overnight scene.

ADA with affected sangfroid: "Hullo, George."

FOTHERINGAY: "Making yourself prettier than ever, eh?"

ADA: "Wish I needn't do it, George. But it has to be done. Lipstick and powder. Why don't you give me a complexion like you gave to Effie? She's dazzling. Considering all you might do, I think you're pretty mean about your miracles."

FOTHERINGAY, holding it for a bit: "Oh! bless you!"

Inaudible instructions and gesture.

Ada becomes much more beautiful.

ADA, still at the mirror: "Now, that's nice, George. Such a becoming wave in the hair, too. Oh, I like little ME. Poised on a delicate neck! I suppose it won't run to a diamond tiara or anything of the sort?"

FOTHERINGAY: *"Well!* Why not?"

Diamond tiara. Ada puts up her hand, incredulously.

FOTHERINGAY: "Look in the glass."

ADA, starts: "Oh, *lovely!* Why, it might be *real.* It's *wonderful."*

FOTHERINGAY: "It *is* real."

ADA: "Oh, yes! Could you do a pearl necklace, George, to go with it? How you do it I *don't* know. It's madness!"

Ada is so absorbed with the pearls in the mirror that she almost forgets Fotheringay.

FOTHERINGAY: "And while we're at it. Why wear that old black dress? 'Ere, let her be dressed in splendid robes like Cleopatra in the play."[21]

---

21. The film's spoken word is "movie" not "play." This alludes to the 1934 Cecil B. DeMille production *Cleopatra,* starring Claudette Colbert. Her sexy costume is the one Mr. Fotheringay dresses Ada Price with. That he mixes up

Transfiguration of Ada Price.

Fotheringay is overwhelmed at the result of his own miracle. Ada stands splendid and triumphant. She doesn't look at Fotheringay. She is exalted by her own effect.

FOTHERINGAY: "Ada, you're wonderful."

ADA: "It's you who are wonderful, Mr. Fotheringay. I never saw anything like it. If Bill could see me now—he'd faint!"

FOTHERINGAY realises with a start that customers are coming into their department. "'Ere's customers coming. They'll see you like that. 'Ere! Ada, be as you were before I changed you!"

ADA becomes the commonplace young woman she was before. She looks into the mirror: "I've gone back. I've gone back. George, did it ever happen?"

Fotheringay is already picking up his boxes again. The customers enter the department escorted by Bill Stoker (floor walking) and Ada rouses herself to serve them. She is still rather distraught and queenly in her manner.

Fotheringay hesitates, looks back at her, hesitates again and goes out of the department, profoundly disturbed.

---

the words for film and stage play in the text illustrates his general lack of sophistication.

PART X

TAKING ADVICE

THE Assistants' sitting-room at Messrs. Grigsby and Blott. It is a not too well furnished apartment, with a small bookcase, horsehair sofa and chairs, table, etc. A clock indicates a quarter past nine. Miss Maggie Hooper is discovered alone with a basket of needlework.

Enter Fotheringay. He stands regarding her.

MISS HOOPER: "And what are *you* doing in the house at this time of night?"

FOTHERINGAY: "I don't know. I just came in. I think I wanted to see you." (He sits down on the sofa.) "Maggie, there's something frightening about this miracle working."

MISS HOOPER: "I told you to get advice about it."

FOTHERINGAY: "I don't get anything *but* advice about it, but it's all different. I don't know where I am. I'm sort of bursting with wonders and I don't dare let 'em loose. There's things happening *in* me, more miraculous than anything happening outside me. I'm beginning to want things—and think of things. I can't tell you. Maggie, I got a *bad* imagination. I got a *dangerous* imagination."[22]

MISS HOOPER: "Well, what did I tell you? You go and see Mr. Maydig. You could see him to-night. He gives people advice in his parlour."

FOTHERINGAY: "I wonder what '*E'll* tell me."

MISS HOOPER: "I've asked you to go and hear him preach time after time. He's wonderful when he really gets going. Seems to lift you up. Takes you right out of yourself."

Dissolve to Mr. Maydig in his study.

---

22. The power to work miracles is beginning to trouble Mr. Fotheringay, even to embarrass him with unbidden carnal fantasies. Frustrated by his failure to command Ada Price to love him (note 13), his long-repressed lust is now surfacing; a "*bad* imagination" he realizes, a dangerously unsettling one. He confesses this to Miss Hooper, a level-headed and healthy-minded associate, but is unable to speak the unspeakable. He now goes to see the Rev. Maydig she recommends and learn of the utopian good he might do. See illustration on page 52.

52 H.G. Wells. *Man Who Could Work Miracles*. Part X

Mr. Fotheringay meets with the Rev. Silas Maydig, from the illustrated story, "The Man Who Could Work Miracles" (1898). In the 1936 film story (and in the 1937 film), this churchman is met with in his private study, minus clerical vestments.

Mr. Maydig is seated in a low arm-chair by the side of a newly-lit fire. He is a long man, with long arms, legs, wrists and neck. He has the fluting voice of an emotional preacher and the normal expression of his face is one of rapture and exaltation. There is a small table convenient to his elbow on which are a number of books, a *Daily Herald* and a weekly paper, *The New Age*, a bottle of whiskey, a syphon and a glass of whisky and soda. The books shown by a momentary close-up are Jean's[23] "Through Space and Time," Temple's "Nature, Man and God," Dunne's "Serial Universe," Weatherhead's "Psychology and Life," and G. D. H. and M. I. Cole's "Guide to Modern Politics."

Mr. Maydig appears to be reading Bertrand Russell's "Freedom and Organisation."

He holds the book in one long hand and gesticulates with the other. He is not so much reading as making his own commentary. Indeed he is hardly reading at all; the book is merely a stimulant.

MAYDIG: "Ah—ah! Wonderful, wonderful. 'To take this sorry scheme of things entire and mould it better to the heart's desire.' Yes, my dear friends, my dearly beloved friends, this poor disordered world, this rich and marvellous world. Do you ever... No! Do we ever—No, no, no. When do we ever lift up our eyes from the things—the sordid urgent little things about us—think—dream—dream of what the world might be? Not bad that;—Dream of what the world might be. If only we had the power—if only we had the faith to do that..."

There is a knock at the door and his housekeeper appears.

"There's a young man, sir, very anxious to see you. Name of Fotheringay. Says it's urgent."

MAYDIG considers: "Fotheringay?—Don't know him. Respectable? Not—a mendicant?"

HOUSEKEEPER: "Nothing of that sort. But he's in some trouble, sir, says he wants advice."

MAYDIG: "Show him in then—show him in. I never refuse myself— if it's like that. Always ready to give what I *can* give."

---

23. Should be Jeans's, re Sir James Jeans (*d*. 1946), the English mathematician and astronomer. Mr. Maydig reads Wells-approved books but has only a vacuous understanding of them, a Wellsian dig at the clergy. It takes a professor of physics in the story's finale, at note 43, to warn Mr. Fotheringay how dangerous is his threat to stop the earth's rotation. But Mr. Fotheringay, in his new-found hubris, pays no need. Instantly the world ends. Miracles or no miracles, he has not the power to go contrariwise to nature without disastrous consequences: a comical little man, ignorant and unworthy of power to the last, who destroys the planet and all on it.

The housekeeper goes out and Maydig puts whisky, syphon, etc., out of sight, after a hasty drink at the whisky. Rearranges books to make their titles more evident. Stands on hearthrug to receive his visitor. Raises himself on his toes. Looms impressively. Enter Fotheringay rather diffidently.

MAYDIG: "Well, sir, what can I do for you?"

FOTHERINGAY: "I'm told you sometimes give good advice to people—and I've got a peculiar sort of trouble—if you can call it a trouble—which perhaps a minister like yourself—"

MAYDIG: "Go on."

FOTHERINGAY: "Well, something very extraordinary has happened to me. I used to think I couldn't do anything. Now—I begin to find I can do just whatever I want to do—by will power."

MAYDIG: "What do you mean, will power?"

FOTHERINGAY: "Work miracles."

MAYDIG: "Miracles!"

FOTHERINGAY: "Ye-eah, miracles—no end of them!"

MAYDIG regards his caller profoundly. "My dear sir—are you by any chance mad? There are no such things as miracles under the present dispensation, I can assure you."

FOTHERINGAY: "Would you think differently—if I worked one?"

MAYDIG: "Well—I'd think it over. I have an open mind. Nobody can deny me that."

FOTHERINGAY: "'Ere goes—what shall it be? Make something appear, eh? Oh! I'm sick of messing about with rabbits and kittens and bunches of flowers. 'Ere! let there be a panther 'ere—a *real* panther—on the hearthrug."

A panther appears crouching between the two men. Maydig starts back and upsets his little table. Fotheringay is evidently also alarmed at the quality of the animal produced. The beast itself is as frightened as either of them. It is on the defensive. It crouches close to the floor and turns its head from one to the other snarling dangerously; then it leaps forward and swings round so as to face them both with its back to the audience, filling up the greater part of the picture.

The voice of FOTHERINGAY is heard: "'Ere! Vanish. Cease to exist."

The panther vanishes and Maydig and Fotheringay confront each other across a crumpled hearthrug.

FOTHERINGAY: "How's that for a miracle?"

MAYDIG recovering slowly: "Something wonderful—yes. A miracle, no!"

FOTHERINGAY: "You mean—there wasn't a real panther 'ere a minute ago?"

MAYDIG: "No, my dear sir. No. Joint hallucination. The thing is quite well known."

FOTHERINGAY: "That panther was an hallucination! 'Ere! I'll bring it back."

MAYDIG: "No! don't do that. But—"

FOTHERINGAY: "Look at these paw marks on the floor. See? Hallucinations don't leave footsteps like that, do they?"

MAYDIG: "I'm willing to be convinced. Yes—yes. There *are* paw marks. Some large carnivore." (His last resistances vanish.) "And you find you really can do things like that? You know Mr.—Mr.—"

FOTHERINGAY: "Fotheringay."

MAYDIG: "Mr. Fotheringay, that was a miracle you did just now. You needn't have any further doubts about it. It was a miracle. Can you do—many other things—of the same sort?"

FOTHERINGAY: "That's what I want to consult you about, Mr. Maydig. I can do all sorts of things. I can heal people. I can clear things up and set things right. I can change things into other things. I can move things about. I don't seem able to get into the insides of people's minds, so to speak, but except for that there doesn't seem to be a limit—not a limit to what I can do."

MAYDIG, head on one side—dreaming expression—grasping the facts. "It's Power."

FOTHERINGAY: "Yes. But what am I going to *do* about it? What would you do about it if you were me? What would *anyone* do? You know, Mr. Maydig, it's a most remarkable thing, before I knew I could work miracles I thought I knew everything I wanted—and wasn't going to get it. And now I can, in a manner of speaking, have everything—something seems to hold me back." He leaves off, doubtful if Maydig is listening.

MAYDIG still getting hold of the vast idea: "Power. Pow-er. My dear young man, what might you not do—what may you not do with the world? Healing! Have you thought?"

He lays a bony hand on Fotheringay's shoulder and points the lone forefinger of the other at vacancy. "Why not banish disease from the world? Do in one swoop, what science and medicine have been toiling to do little by little! A world without disease."

FOTHERINGAY: "I hadn't thought of that. I thought I'd just go about and cure somebody here and somebody there."

MAYDIG: "Sweep it *all* away. A world glowing with health—newborn.

"The world's great age begins anew.

"The golden years return.

"The earth doth like a snake renew her winter weeds outworn.[24] And then peace! You can give them plenty—make corn, power yield a thousandfold. What is there left to fight about?"

FOTHERINGAY: "You don't think there may be a catch in it somewhere?"

MAYDIG: "What catch?"

FOTHERINGAY: "I think I'd rather go gradually for a bit. When you get on the big side—it's unexpected sometimes. That panther—"

MAYDIG with upturned face: "No doubt a certain wise caution is needed, yes. We must go circumspectly. We must harness our panthers. But if we go without haste, let us also go without delay. I see such splendour in this Power of yours, such hope for our race, such starry Hope."

FOTHERINGAY: "Talking of upsetting things, Major Grigsby and Mr. Bampfylde were very anxious I shouldn't upset things. They did seem to think there might be a catch."

MAYDIG: "Those men have limited minds—extremely limited minds. I have never been able to work with either of them."

FOTHERINGAY sticking to his subject: "You see, what Mr. Bampfylde said was that all human beings are held together by money really and by wanting money and things, and that if they didn't want they wouldn't have anything to do."

MAYDIG: "I find that intolerable. I find that absolutely intolerable. Have they no faith in Man?" He hovers over Fotheringay, enforcing his remarks with gestures of his hands. "Is there no art? Is there no beauty? Are there not boundless seas of knowledge yet unplumbed?"

FOTHERINGAY: "Mr. Bampfylde didn't seem to think they were likely to go in for that sort of thing all at once."

MAYDIG: "Because the man has no imagination. Because he has no soul. Because he has forgotten the clouds of glory he trailed from heaven in his infancy. The business man! The banker! Save me from them! Man bankrupt—in a world of plenty!"

FOTHERINGAY: "I suppose reely, they *ought* to find a better way of managing things."

MAYDIG: "Of course! But will they ever trouble to do so—until they are compelled? Until things overtake them? No, sir. And that is where

---

24. Wells uses this occasion to correct his own mistake when he misquoted Shelley in his epigraph to *In the Days of the Comet* (1906a), one of the scientific romances in which gas from a passing comet miraculously transforms human society overnight; instant Wellsian utopia. There he takes Shelley's line to read, "The Earth doth like a Snake renew/ her Winter Skin outworn." Maydig then cites Wordsworth's "clouds of glory" trailed by man from his divine origins, but for Wells man makes himself out of his ape-like ancestry.

we begin. To-morrow. Suppose now—every poor soul in the world found a five-pound note or its equivalent in hand—suddenly. So that they could go out and buy things! Just think of that! Just think of the effect of it."

FOTHERINGAY: "I'd like to do that. If you're sure there's no catch in it. But it will give Mr. Bampfylde fits."

MAYDIG: "Convulsions, I hope—convulsions! And then—healing. All over the world. Everyone suddenly saying 'Ha! Ha! I feel well. I feel strong.'"

FOTHERINGAY: "I don't see any harm in that."

MAYDIG: "Nor I."

FOTHERINGAY: "It might put the doctors out a bit."

MAYDIG: "And why?"

FOTHERINGAY: "Naturally they think it *their* business to keep us healthy—"

MAYDIG: "Oh Heaven! Oh Spirit of Righteousness! Are we to remain needy to please the bankers and business men, and unhealthy to provide fees for the doctors?"

FOTHERINGAY: "I only thought it made things a bit complicated."

MAYDIG: "Well, well. Sleep on it first. We shall have to provide for the doctors and traders—yes, I admit that. It cannot all be done in a flash. There's an inertia in things that has to be considered. I will think and think and think. I shan't sleep, Mr. Fotheringay. Not a wink. I shall keep vigil. The last night of human misery! The pause before the Dawn. What a glorious thought. Will *you* be able to sleep?"

FOTHERINGAY: "Well, I've had a pretty busy day."

MAYDIG: "You are one of God's innocents. You will sleep. And yet I can hardly bear to part like this. Let us do *one simple* good thing before we go to bed to-night—an earnest of all we mean to do. Now let us think. Some little thing. Ah! There is my neighbour here, Colonel Winstanley. Chairman of the Bench—full of influence and all that influence against progress.[25] Always treated me with the utmost incivility. I bear

---

25. That is, the Colonel is chief magistrate of his district, an honorary title given conspicuous members of the local gentry, always unprogressive in Wells. Here Mr. Maydig agrees with him, for all of Wells's anticlerical prejudice: another example of the film story's ironic and ambiguous artistic subtleties.

Col. Winstanley is the Boss of Dewhinton as Rudolf is the military Boss of Everytown in *Things to Come*, although he has only a few deferential policemen to order about. He illustrates the traditional master-man relationship mentioned in note 40, even as he bosses his personal servant Moody.

him no malice. He sits late at night and drinks—drinks, I fear, too much. I am no pedant in these matters, but *he*—boozes. He will be sitting now, with his decanter beside him. Change it to some simple non-intoxicating fluid. And all his house is decorated with swords and weapons. Beat them into plough-shares. Turns his swords to reaping-hooks."

FOTHERINGAY: "But will he like it?"

MAYDIG: "Not at first. But it will set him thinking."

FOTHERINGAY, a little reluctantly: "Well, I would like to do something before I turn in. Colonel Winstanley, you said? 'Ere goes." Gesture and inaudible command.

Another example of the type is Major Grigsby (note 16), dominator of subservient shop assistants like Mr. Fotheringay. But when power comes to this ludicrous little man, he reverts to the same old style of dominance.

PART XI

THE PACIFICATION OF COLONEL WINSTANLEY

THE hall of the house of Colonel Winstanley.[26] It is decorated with the heads of two tigers and a number of spearheads, kreeses, swords and similar weapons. A bell is heard ringing in gusts. An anxious-looking butler without a tie, buttoning up a coat he has just put on, hurries across the hall. The camera follows him across a large dark conventional drawing-room to the study of the colonel. The colonel is revealed in a mess-jacket standing before an arm-chair beside an open fire with a glass of whisky in his hand and an expression of strong distaste on his face. He is a fine good-looking old soldier, but choler and intolerance are in his blood. He sips and eyes his butler accusingly.

BUTLER: "You rang, sir?"

COLONEL: "I rang six times. You go to bed too soon, Moody. And now, tell me; what the *devil's* the matter with this whisky? It's gone wrong. It's lost its taste. It's flat. It's worse than flat. It's mawkish, I tell you—mawkish. What have you been doing to it? Have you been watering it, Moody? It isn't even whisky!"

BUTLER: "It's the real old stuff, sir. Out of the old jar."

COLONEL: "It's *not* the real old stuff, and it's *not* out of the old jar. It's got no fire. It's got no guts. What have you been doing to it?"

BUTLER: "I can assure you, sir—"

COLONEL: "Do you mean to assure me I'm drinking whisky when I know I'm not!"

A frightful clatter of metal falling interrupts the conversation.

---

26. In the 1937 film he is played by Ralph Richardson, his second film appearance. The first was as the Boss of Everytown in *Things to Come*, played with the same bluster, but always with very controlled and interesting body language and business. Richardson (*d.* 1983) started out as a stage actor and was knighted in 1953 for his outstanding career. His role as Colonel Winstanley in *Miracles*, the London film production, is such a remarkable performance that the video tape from Vintage Classics (MGM) is worth getting to watch just for that: but not to overlook Wells's masterful scenario and dialogue.

COLONEL: "What the devil is *that*? What's happening? First I get water instead of whisky and next the house falls down. Something has happened to the collection. Go and see, man. Go and see. Don't stand staring there."

Exit butler.

The COLONEL returns to his whisky. "It's POISON. I'm being poisoned! Pah! Moody, there! What's happened out there? Why don't you come and tell me?"

The butler's footsteps heard hurrying through drawing-room.

Re-enter butler, leaving the drawing-room door open. His expression is one of horror and amazement and he carries a sickle in his hand.

He speaks slowly: "I don't understand, sir. When I crossed the hall three minutes ago everything seemed as right as could be. And now—it's frightful."

COLONEL: "What's frightful? Speak up, man, what's frightful?"

BUTLER: "The collection, sir—the whole collection."

COLONEL: "Go on, go on!"

BUTLER: "The collection, practically all the collection—well—it's gone, sir."

COLONEL: "*Gone!*"

BUTLER: "Yessir, all the swords have gone—the whole collection, and there's a lot of other things—look like agricultural implements to me, sir—mostly on the floor. This, sir, for example."

Butler holds out a sickle with manifest distaste and the Colonel takes and examines it.

COLONEL in a tone of wonder: "What's this—this blinking Bolshevik thing?[27] What *is* it? What does it mean? Is the house going mad? My swords gone! Gone? What are you saying? I don't understand. Let's have a look at 'em."

Scene changes to hall of the Colonel's house. Colonel and butler survey a scene of wreckage. The Colonel's collection has undergone a

---

27. A reference is made to the hammer and sickle flag of the Soviet Union. The Colonel is made out to be horribly reactionary for his anticommunist contempt. The film's audience, in England, would have understood that Wells had his éclat for being the Soviet Union's chief apologist, then a popular stance. Wells, however, took issue with the regime's dishonest Marxist ideology, something *not* widely understood.

The Colonel's treasured weapons collection he no doubt collected while serving the British Raj in India against fierce hill tribesmen. Or maybe also in one of the British colonial possessions in tribal Africa.

complete transformation into plough-shares and reaping-hooks, and most of it is littered on the floor.

After a speechless moment the COLONEL shouts: "If I could lay my hands on the FOOL who did this! Are there no police in Dewhinton? The fellow must have come right in as I was sitting there. He's stolen my swords! I understand that. But what he means by leaving this—this *muck*, beats me."

The outdoor bell rings.

COLONEL: "And who's ringing at this time of night?"

BUTLER: "Can't imagine, sir."

COLONEL: "*Don't* imagine. Go and see! If somebody's trying some sort of game on *me*—!"

Butler opens the outer door. Superintendent Smithells and Constable Thumble appear hesitatingly. The superintendent has a telegram in his hand.

COLONEL, frantic: "*You!* Look at this! Look at this mess here. My swords—my collection. Do you know anything about it? Come in, confound you. Don't stand gaping there on the doorstep. It's just been done. Come in and see what's happened to my weapons!"

The superintendent and constable come in slowly and heavily and stare in perplexity at the litter in the hall. Then they look at each other portentously and deeply.

COLONEL barks: "Well?"

SUPERINTENDENT: "It's some more of it."

COLONEL: "More of *what*?"

SUPERINTENDENT: "These—miracles."

Colonel Winstanley seems on the verge of great eloquence but happily for the censorship finds himself speechless.

SUPERINTENDENT: "There's been a serious outbreak of miracles in the district, sir. Quite beyond anyone's experience."

COLONEL: "Miracles!"

SUPERINTENDENT: "Yessir, miracles."

COLONEL: "There aren't such things."

SUPERINTENDENT: "Not properly, sir. Which makes it so disconcerting, sir. We didn't come disturbing you at this time of night about nothing. But seeing, sir, as you are the Chairman of the Bench, we thought you might be able to help—"

COLONEL: "What is it now? What is it?"

SUPERINTENDENT: "It's about this Constable Winch of ours, what's been missing since last night. We've searched everywhere. We've dragged the millstream. We've made enquiries up and down the railway line."

COLONEL: "You don't expect me to find him for you at ten minutes to midnight, do you?"

SUPERINTENDENT: "No sir. But we've got a cable."

COLONEL: "What's the good of a cable?"[28]

SUPERINTENDENT: "A telegram, sir—from San Francisco."

COLONEL: "Oh! Is *that* it?" Seizes the telegram. Reads:

"Reply paid. 36 words. Police Dewhinton Essex Eng. Is Constable Winch missing stop has appeared mysteriously here stop slightly injured in street riot provoked by himself stop alleged miracle stop accuses one Fotheringay stop any information and instructions for disposal of Constable cable private and exclusive to Will Prackman Office S.F. Stop. All charges to me."

COLONEL: "This is some sort of hoax."

SUPERINTENDENT: "With all due respect, sir, it isn't a hoax. It's something more serious. It's that young fellow, Fotheringay."

COLONEL: "Fotheringay! I must have a whisky. If I can't have a whisky my mind will give way."

BUTLER: "Yessir—but—"

COLONEL: "Good *Lord*! Is that another miracle?"

BUTLER: "I'll get another jar, sir—I'll get one with the seal unbroken."

Shift scene to the Colonel's study. The butler is breaking the seal and uncorking a four-gallon jar of whisky. The others stand round stupefied but still faintly hopeful. Four glasses are filled—neat. There is no trifling with soda-water. Four men taste together and put their glasses down. Their faces are very grave.

COLONEL breaking the silence: "Soap and water."

SUPERINTENDENT: "It's nastier than that, sir. I should say it was one of those temperance drinks."

COLONEL: "Well, Moody, anything to say?"

BUTLER: "Sir, I got my weaknesses. But I'd as soon poison a baby as tamper with whisky."

SUPERINTENDENT: "If you ask me—it's Fotheringay again."

COLONEL: "Fotheringay! More Fotheringay. I'll keep calm. I owe it to myself and everyone to keep calm. Oh! perfectly calm. I'll see the fellow to-morrow. No fuss. I'll just talk to him. Quietly. Calmly. No good getting heated. I'll have it out with him. You bring him to me, sort of

---

28. The Colonel is just as ignorant of things in general as Mr. Fotheringay. He thinks a "cable" is a long rope, and has to be told by the superintendent of police that it means a telegram (sent overland from San Francisco to New York and thence by undersea transatlantic cable to England).

casually, Smithells. Just for a bit of advice. In my garden. Don't alarm him.... And keep your eye on him while you're bringing him. Have your truncheon up your sleeve. If he lifts a finger. If he so much as *looks* like New Zealand or Tokio—*club* him. *I'll* see you through."

The COLONEL reflects: "No, I won't see him to-night. Open air. Open daylight. When you can watch his eyes and hands. One man to another."

PART XII

THE COLONEL PLEADS

THE Colonel's rose-garden. It is an old-fashioned pleasant garden with specimen trees and a monkey-puzzle in the background. Glimpse of the house. Bright sunshine. The COLONEL is in white, with a Panama straw hat, and he carries an instrument for rooting up dandelions and plantains without stooping. But he is not weeding his lawn. He paces up and down, weeder behind him. A sleepless night has done nothing to tranquillise him. He exhorts himself: "Handle the situation firmly, calmly. Don't *shout*. Don't get excited. Study your man. Grim if you like, but no bluster. Ah!"

Superintendent and Fotheringay appear approaching.

COLONEL WINSTANLEY: "So that's the miracle worker, eh? Don't look it—I must say. Little cad. Spoilt my whisky, smashed my collection. Don't get excited! The firm hand! Well, Mr. Superintendent, is this the young man you wanted me to see?"

SUPERINTENDENT: "This is Mr. Fotheringay, sir—as directed."

FOTHERINGAY'S manner is a mixture of habitual social deference and a new-found assurance. "*At* your service, sir."

COLONEL WINSTANLEY: "I want a talk with you. I want a serious talk with you. As Chairman of the Bench and Deputy Lieutenant, *and* the former owner of a valuable collection of weapons, *and* the proprietor of a once powerful cellar, *and* the organiser of the Society for the Preservation of Law and Social Discipline here, and a fellow-citizen of our unfortunate constable, Winch, I naturally and properly want a talk with you. I want, if I may say so, an explanation—"

FOTHERINGAY: "*How*—I wish I knew. *Why*—it's almost as hard. All I know is I seem able to do things."

COLONEL WINSTANLEY: "And nice friendly things you do, eh?"

FOTHERINGAY: "Well, you see—it's difficult to know what to do without offending people."

COLONEL WINSTANLEY: "Offending people! How the devil else could I take that trick about my whisky and my collection?"

FOTHERINGAY: "Well, Mr. Maydig—"

COLONEL WINSTANLEY: "Maydig—that new preacher chap! How does *he* come in?"

FOTHERINGAY: "Well, he was advising me."

COLONEL WINSTANLEY: "He was advising you!"

FOTHERINGAY: "And he thought for once if you went to bed sober—"

COLONEL WINSTANLEY: "Would you please say that again?"

FOTHERINGAY: "Well, if you didn't have too much to drink—"

COLONEL WINSTANLEY: "Go on, sir. Go on. I can bear it. I want to hear you out."

FOTHERINGAY: "And if we kind of made a symbolical change of all those swords of yours, it would sort of prepare your mind for the Peace of the World."

COLONEL WINSTANLEY: "And when may that be due?"

FOTHERINGAY: "Oh, almost at once—Peace—Plenty. Mr. Maydig made it very clear how we were to set about it."

COLONEL WINSTANLEY: "And you're going to set about it—when?"

FOTHERINGAY: "I'm going to see him about twelve and I suppose we shall start the Golden Age[29] somewhen in the afternoon."

The COLONEL has become ominously calm. He speaks to the garden. "They are going to start the Golden Age somewhen—this afternoon." He addresses himself to the sky and universe, and speaks with great deliberation: "They ... are ... going ... to ... start ... the ... Golden ... Age ... somewhen ... this ... afternoon."

He turns to Fotheringay. "Under the circumstances I hardly like to mention my collection and my whisky."

FOTHERINGAY: "Don't mention it. We reely didn't mean to annoy. I'll put it right now." Gesture and inaudible words.

COLONEL WINSTANLEY: "Is that all you do? Just that?"

FOTHERINGAY: "That's all."

COLONEL WINSTANLEY: "And the miracle done. And my whisky is whisky. And the collection back."

FOTHERINGAY: "We can go and see it. The extraordinary thing is I *can* do these things. I could turn this garden into a palm tree forest and fill it with tigers. There reely doesn't seem to be a limit to what I can do."

The COLONEL surveying him: "There isn't a limit to what you can do! *You!*"

---

29. In harking back to the Golden Age of classical mythology, Mr. Fotheringay reveals that he is no socialist. All socialists, pre–Marxist (like Wells) or later, projected utopia into the future, not as a recovery of some ideal from the past.

FOTHERINGAY: "Me. It just comes out of me."

COLONEL WINSTANLEY: "You can do practically anything?"

FOTHERINGAY: "Well, would you like me to do anything?"

The COLONEL aghast: "But a fellow of your sort!"[30]

FOTHERINGAY, betraying a latent irritation: "Well, why shouldn't it be a fellow of my sort? Do you *want* to see a miracle? Something big?"

COLONEL WINSTANLEY: "Perhaps it's just as well to know what one is up against."

FOTHERINGAY: "Like to see India again? Like a glimpse of—what's some Indian place? Bombay. Let us both be in Bombay."

Scene changes to a crowded place in Bombay.

FOTHERINGAY: "Well, Colonel?"

COLONEL WINSTANLEY rubs his eyes: "You can do a thing like this?"

FOTHERINGAY: "Nobody else did it. Are you satisfied you are in Bombay?"

COLONEL WINSTANLEY: "The place has changed a lot. But I recognise it. Yes, I admit it; we're in Bombay. And how the devil we shall get back, Heaven knows. I had to talk to some men after lunch."

FOTHERINGAY: "Very well. You shall talk to them. We won't stay here. Let us be back in the Colonel's garden at Dewhinton. Now."

They return to the garden scene.

FOTHERINGAY: "Well, sir? Is it all right, can I work miracles or can't I?"

COLONEL WINSTANLEY: "No doubt of it. Talk about abolishing distance!"[31]

They move towards the house in silence.

Dissolve as they go up the garden.

The scene changes to the hall of the Colonel's house. Everything is in order. The Colonel and Fotheringay are continuing a conversation

---

30. The Colonel is mocked for his class prejudice, but Wells shares it. Mr. Fotheringay is indeed not the sort of fellow to be trusted with power. He is Vishnu incarnate, the Hindu divinity the Wellsian elect in *Things to Come* suppress. In the next convincing miracle, Mr. Fotheringay takes the Colonel back to India, an association that resonates with the film story's theme and theory regarding the Hindu trinity.

31. Alludes to a favorite Wellsian phrase, "the abolition of distance," recurrent from *Anticipations* (1902) onward. He anticipated today's global village piety, seeing that air travel would make for globalization. From that he concluded the need for a world state.

that has evidently been going on for some time. The Colonel is sitting on a hall table. Fotheringay stands still or walks a little to and fro.

FOTHERINGAY: "Mr. Maydig, you see, he has Ideas. He has Imagination. Now there isn't much sense—seeing these Gifts that have come to me—in going on with business and banking and all that. Mr. Maydig calls that a Want System—and now we are going to live in a Plenty System. There's no need for people to be hard up now. No need for people to be sick and ill and hungry. No need for robbing and cheating. And no need for war."

COLONEL WINSTANLEY: "No need for *anything* so far as I can see."

FOTHERINGAY: "Well, it will be *different*. But Mr. Maydig says you can't work miracles and stay as you are."

COLONEL WINSTANLEY: "And if you put an end to war, sir,—as I gather you intend to do before tea-time to-day—and I am beginning to believe you can—if you put an end to competition,[32] make work unnecessary, give everybody more money than they can spend, then I ask you: What are people going to DO, sir? What are they going to *do*?"

FOTHERINGAY, simply and candidly: "You know that's where *I'm* puzzled. But Mr. Maydig, he thinks we ought to just go about Loving one another."

This is too much for COLONEL WINSTANLEY. He jumps down from the table and roars: "Go about *loving* one another! Go about *loving* one another! Are you mad, sir? Are you human? Have you no sense of decency? The most private—the most sacred feelings!"

FOTHERINGAY: "Mr. Maydig seemed to see it so differently. Of course, there's art and science and making things."

COLONEL WINSTANLEY: "Fretwork and—" He gasps apoplectically. "Fretwork and foolery!"

FOTHERINGAY: "I suppose we can give it a trial. We don't properly know what human beings *will* do, Mr. Maydig says."

---

32. The Colonel of course favors private-profit capitalism as Wells does not. A competitive, free-market economy is abolished under Wellsian state capitalism. But the colonel's apprehension as to what people would *do* with their lives under such a system of plenty is on the mark. He hears Mr. Fotheringay report that Mr. Maydig says people would "just go about Loving one another." But this is *not* what Wells himself had in mind for his utopian world state: the mere prelude to the conquest of outer space and the ongoing extension of humanity amidst the stars to ensure racial immortality.

In the event, Mr. Fotheringay does not heed Mr. Maydig and follows the selfish inclinations of Vishnu in his petty heart.

COLONEL WINSTANLEY gives way to rage. "Mr. Maydig says! Mr. Maydig says! And you're launching this bedlam millennium of yours in about six hours from now. What is going to happen to us all? What will become of us?"

FOTHERINGAY: "I reely don't know exactly myself. It'll be a bit of a change. Mr. Maydig says—"

COLONEL's frantic gesture: "Oh!" He walks some steps from Fotheringay, glances at a particularly sinister Malay kreese on the wall, hesitates for a moment and then by a great effort of self-control comes back to parley with Fotheringay.

COLONEL WINSTANLEY: "Now, look here, Mr. Fotheringay, won't you give all this business a few hours'—a few days' consideration, before you—before you let rip. Here we are. We've built up a sort of civilisation. People fit into it."

FOTHERINGAY: "Not so perfectly."

COLONEL WINSTANLEY: "At any rate they get along. We've got the Empire. A kind of order."

FOTHERINGAY: "That's all very well for people like you. But most people in the world are people like me. It's natural for you to want to keep things as they are. But I'm all for letting them loose. See? I don't *mind* change. I think change may be a Lark."

COLONEL WINSTANLEY: "Hasn't there been enough change in the last hundred years, railways, electricity, photography, steel ships, radio?"

FOTHERINGAY; "It's shook us up a bit but it hasn't killed us. I'm all for More and Better Change."[33]

---

33. All good things in Wells, and "More and Better Change," as Mr. Fotheringay says, is indeed progressive, but not in the way he envisions.

PART XIII

MAN OF ACTION

THE scene is the Colonel's study. It is afternoon. The Colonel has changed his garden clothes and is smoking a cigar. With him are Grigsby, Bampfylde, the Superintendent of Police, a vicar, a young gentleman in a very horsy get-up. They have been given coffee, cigars, liqueurs and after lunch refreshment.

The Colonel in a state of plethoric excitement, dominates the scene. But the others are in substantial agreement with him.

COLONEL WINSTANLEY: "You don't seem to see how serious it all is! While we are sitting here in our old homes and our old habits and following our old ways, these two dangerous lunatics are going to change the world—change us and everything. Can anything stay as it was? I ask you. You know their business ideas, Grigsby?"

GRIGSBY: "He'll kill business."

BAMPFYLDE: "He'll kill credit. The human world is held together by a cash nexus and if that goes—everything goes."

COLONEL WINSTANLEY: "And he'll leave the country open and unarmed to anyone who chooses to start an air raid.[34] This measly-looking little draper chap is the most dangerous lunatic that ever got loose. I tell you, Mr. Smithells,—law or no law—you'll have to arrest him."

SUPERINTENDENT: "Well—if I try it—? Motor criminals are bad enough for the local constabulary, but if we are to deal with *miracle* criminals. It's beyond us—Colonel, and I warn you."

The COLONEL now becomes most important and the camera comes towards a close-up. "It's beyond us."

"Well, I'm all for law and order—under normal conditions.

"But are these normal conditions? Sometimes there is such a thing as drastic action or none. Sometimes still—a man must take a risk and

---

34. Alludes to the build up of the German air fleet under Hitler after he took power in 1933, while Britain remained defenseless. The air raids begin in *Things to Come*, as in fact they later did.

break the law. Gentlemen, I don't ask you to share my responsibilities. Only maybe *later*—"

The Colonel's face takes on a look of stern resolution.

"These men are mad dogs. They have to be treated like mad dogs. It is our world and all that is worth while—against their confounded antics.

"If one happens to see red—if one happens to see red.

"There's such a thing as justification."

He turns away and the camera comes round to see him walk out of the room, and follows him as he strides down the hall, receding down a vista. No one moves until Bampfylde stirs and nods slowly and understandingly to Grigsby. Then both look at the superintendent, who remains enigmatic at attention. The vicar affects to be lost in thought. The young sportsman cranes his neck to follow the Colonel's movements.

The back of the Colonel is seen looking at a sporting gun on the wall. Then very deliberately he takes it down and examines it. But it will not do. No. He wants a bullet, not buckshot. He gets down a service rifle. He goes to a cabinet and takes out cartridges. Sharp clicks as he loads the gun. All this is done with his back to the audience. Fade out.

PART XIV

DOUBTS ON THE EVE OF THE MILLENNIUM

SCENERY. Some very pleasant sunlit meadows near Dewhinton. A river. Willow trees, running water and Dewhinton church amidst a clump of elms in the distance.

Enter Maydig and Fotheringay walking in a leisurely fashion. Maydig leads and talks. Fotheringay conveys an effect of being drawn along after him.

MAYDIG: "What a perfect afternoon! And to think it is New Year's Eve for the world. We are on the verge of the greatest change this Earth of Ours has ever seen. Want will vanish and Plenty reign. Ring out the Old, Ring in the New.... You know it is just as though I wanted to loiter a little—before the beginning and the End."

They sit down on a fallen log.

MAYDIG: "Silly old world, what a lesson you have to learn!"

FOTHERINGAY: "I wish I knew a bit more exactly what we are going to do. Last night I was thinking a lot. I'm not *clear* on all sorts of things yet."

MAYDIG: "Nor I. It is all one great shining cloud of hope."

FOTHERINGAY: "Yes. But I have to do my miracles in a sort of order—one after the other."

MAYDIG: "I realise that."

FOTHERINGAY: "There's this making everybody in the world perfectly healthy. I suppose that's all right?"

MAYDIG: "Gloriously, exuberantly healthy, why not?"

FOTHERINGAY: "Well. They'll bounce about a bit. I suppose you *can* have human bodies perfectly healthy—and they'll still work?"

MAYDIG: "Certainly. Why not? Drawn by pleasure instead of driven by pain."

FOTHERINGAY: "What is perfectly healthy?"

MAYDIG: "We shall see."

FOTHERINGAY: "The doctors won't like it. It's *their* business to make us healthy. They won't like us to cut in on them."

MAYDIG: "Don't tell me, Mr. Fotheringay, don't tell me! Don't tell me that doctors do not want the whole world to be one glowing mass of health."

FOTHERINGAY: "Do I *need* to tell you? Those doctors—they'll have nothing left but their appetites."

Maydig features moral horror.

FOTHERINGAY: "But it's all like that. People are used to living in a certain way. That's what Mr. Grigsby and Mr. Bampfylde mean. If we give everybody plenty of money and plenty of everything—won't it be a bit like winning without playing a game? What are people going to DO?"

MAYDIG: "There will be plenty to do—plenty."

FOTHERINGAY: "What?"

MAYDIG: "Oh! we can arrange property and production and trade and money so that there will still be plenty of things to do."

FOTHERINGAY: "Yes, but we haven't settled how we are going to do that."

MAYDIG: "Matters of detail. And then as to this question of leisure. It's been raised already by science and invention and rationalisation and all that. It's not a *new* question. You and your miracles are only hurrying things on a bit. Scientific progress has warned us already. The answer is the intelligent pursuit of happiness, artistic work, creative energy."[35]

FOTHERINGAY: "But that's where the Colonel comes in. Mr. Maydig, d'you think people—people as a general rule—want to go in for artistic work and all that?"

MAYDIG: "We must *make* them want."

FOTHERINGAY: "That's just where *my* miracles stop. I can't get *inside* people; I've tried it a bit. I can turn them upside down, send them to San Francisco in a jiffy, heal their diseases, make them rich—but people remain people."

MAYDIG: "An individual remains an individual."

FOTHERINGAY: "I suppose that's how you'd put it."

MAYDIG: "But you can affect them indirectly. Healthier people are happier people. Easier people are kindlier people. People who are not vexed or driven are better."

FOTHERINGAY: "Yes. To a certain extent. To a certain extent. But then won't a lot of new—desires get loose? Mr. Maydig, I've got some powerful desires. As I feel this power in me, they seem to grow."

---

35. While Mr. Maydig is progressive enough for Wells, his idealized end, happiness and creative art, is not Wells's. He rather envisions unending work to build a utopian future that is forever distant, always Becoming, never Being.

MAYDIG: "Ah, my young friend! How often it has been my lot to hear that confession from young men in their strength. I know. I understand. We all have those powerful desires. Even in my own case—"[36]

His expression is of one who experiences a rush of memories.

FOTHERINGAY: "Never mind about *your* case. It's *my* case I'm talking about."

MAYDIG: "I can assure you there is nothing singular about you."

FOTHERINGAY: "Exactly. That's where the trouble will come in. If everybody's like me—"

MAYDIG: "The guidance, the mastery of desire is a pure love."

FOTHERINGAY: "I *got* a pure love."

MAYDIG: "Then?"

FOTHERINGAY: "It isn't enough. There's that girl Maggie Hooper, who told me to come along and see you."

MAYDIG: "I know her. A very pure, simple, sensible girl."

FOTHERINGAY: "That's her. I'm very fond of her. That's all right. But the girl—the sort of girl that sets me *wanting*, isn't her."

He stands up.

MAYDIG: "Dear, dear! Wandering of desire. You must restrain it."

FOTHERINGAY: "Well, why *should* I? I happen to want a girl called Ada Price. Maggie sews on my buttons and mends my socks. She's perfectly lovely when she is sewing on buttons and mending socks. But there's a sort of 'Come and Take me' about Ada Price—"

MAYDIG also standing and assuming a pulpit manner: "The trouble is as old as the hills. Resist temptation. Let your motto be Service."[37]

FOTHERINGAY: "Why should it be? *Why* Service? Why should *I* go about making people healthy and beautiful and get nothing out of it? Why should I let Bill Stoker, blast him, get away with it?"

MAYDIG: "My *dear* Friend!"

FOTHERINGAY: "And that's what most people are going to say! All this Power—it's going to let me loose. All these miracles of Speed and Plenty and Health, they're going to let most people loose. 'Come and Take me'—*that* stirs us."

---

36. Mr. Maydig truly understands the "*bad* imagination" Mr. Fotheringay clumsily confesses to Miss Hooper (note 22).

37. The spirit of Vishnu in Mr. Fotheringay drives him to ignore this altruistic motto. He still lusts after Ada Price, and will get her one way or the other.

PART XV

DEATH COMES INTO THE PICTURE

SAME grouping.

A rifle shot is heard. The tearing whine of a bullet follows. Fotheringay's hat flies off and he puts his hand to his head, which is hurt. He stares in astonishment at his blood-stained fingers. The whine of a second bullet follows and a twig of an overhanging tree is shot off.

"They're shooting at us," cries MAYDIG. "Lie down," and he goes promptly flat on his stomach. But Fotheringay remains standing.

FOTHERINGAY: "Stop that! Stop any more bullets."

The blood comes pouring down his cheek.

FOTHERINGAY: "No bullets to hit me. Nothing to hurt me. And the wound on my scalp, stop bleeding and be well again."

But his face and his hand are still smeared with blood and remain so throughout this scene, giving his face a certain forcible strangeness.

FOTHERINGAY: "Me, be invulnerable. See? *Now!* Ah!"

He has thought and realised and changed with great rapidity. From now on, there is real force in his bearing. His last traces of deference and hesitation have gone.

FOTHERINGAY: "And now, let's see who fired that shot. I want a word with him. 'Ere, you over there! Let your gun barrel be solid now!"

He stops. He looks at Maydig who rises slowly on all fours, looking back at him. The two confront each other but they are no longer even pretending to be master and pupil.

FOTHERINGAY: "Stand up, Maydig.... And that's all this silly world can do to a man who can work miracles! Who meant nothing better than to do things for it. Healing their illnesses! Giving them plenty! Making them free! Tried to cheat me out of my life! Tried to stop me. I suppose—" He figures with his finger out before him. "—I suppose another inch would have settled me.... Now let's go and see who did the shooting. I think I can make a pretty good guess."

MAYDIG: "And I."

They start off together. Maydig has the longer legs but something obliges him now to let Fotheringay lead the way.

MAYDIG: "I suppose—wouldn't it be well to make me invulnerable too?"

FOTHERINGAY looks at him for a moment: "All in good time, Maydig. But just for a bit, I'll look after you. So long as I am safe—trust me—everything is safe."

Change to the colonel behind a thick and flowery hedge. Honeysuckle and wild roses. He watches through the branches the two advancing. He shakes his fist at them. Across a broad field Maydig and Fotheringay are seen approaching. The colonel raises his rifle as if to shoot and finds it useless.

COLONEL: "This is too much." He mutters. "Take cover." He throws down his rifle and crouches down.

Return to the grim face of Fotheringay advancing. Then to Maydig behind him. Maydig apprehensive and subdued. They advance, striding nearer and nearer. The top of the hedge comes into the picture. Maydig and Fotheringay look down over the hedge into the field.

FOTHERINGAY: "Where is he?"

Maydig and Fotheringay scramble over and through the hedge and look about them. The colonel has disappeared. His abandoned gun lies on the thick grass.

MAYDIG: "He's fled! At any moment he may shoot again."

FOTHERINGAY: "He can't."

MAYDIG: "I hope most sincerely he can't. If *I* were invulnerable..."

FOTHERINGAY: "But where *is* he?" He looks at the hedge and has a new inspiration. "'Ere! All of you—you roses and honeysuckle and nettles and grass—all of you. Answer. Speak up! Where is he?"

Close-up of the WILD ROSES. They speak in hoarse, thin voices: "He's in the ditch to the left."

Close-up of the NETTLES. They speak in acid tones: "He's in the ditch to the left."

Close-up of the HONEYSUCKLE. Its voice is sweet: "He's in the ditch below me."

Close-up of the GRASS below. A flat herbaceous voice rather like Greta Garbo's: "He's *here*."

The grasses part[38] and the Colonel crawls slowly out of the ditch; remains on all fours for a moment resentfully and then gets up.

---

38. Plants speak and tall grass parts to reveal where the Colonel is hiding after taking a shot at Mr. Fotheringay, grazing his scalp. Nature's obedience to him relates to a point of discussion at the midday meal in the drapery firm's dining room (Part V). Miss Hooper tells how her sprained arm was cured. Bill Stoker responds by saying, "You're like the Spirit of Nature, Fotheringay. But

COLONEL, with a grimace: "*Kamerad!*"

FOTHERINGAY: "I thought it was you. None of the others would have been as outright as that. You are a man of action. I *knew* it was you."

COLONEL: "There's no fighting against miracles. Well, well. You've got to work your silly monkey tricks, I suppose. I tell you I'm sorry I didn't get in with that first shot. And now, get on with Mr. Maydig's magic millennium and see how you like it."

FOTHERINGAY: "No."

COLONEL: "You don't mean to say you've had a gleam of sanity!"

FOTHERINGAY: "I've been learning fast and hard, colonel, for two days. Perhaps there won't be a millennium. Perhaps there can't be. 'Ere's Maydig, he's got no end of ideas ... but I've got my feelings ... and it's me that has to put them through."

MAYDIG: "But you don't mean to give up all the things we've talked about. Just because he tried to shoot you."

FOTHERINGAY: "Not that."

MAYDIG: "And because your own desires are strong!"

FOTHERINGAY: "It isn't only that. Some of your things I shall do and some I shan't. *I* can work miracles—I! It's *me* has the Power. This isn't the world of Colonel Winstanley any more. It isn't the world of Grigsby or Bampfylde or anyone else. And it isn't going to be the world of the Reverend Silas Maydig neither. It's going to be the world of George McWhirter Fotheringay D.G.,[39] and as I want it so it will be, and what I want I get. All of you—you wanted just to use me. Now I'm going to use myself."

MAYDIG: "What for?"

FOTHERINGAY: "For getting exactly what I fancy. That's the natural human thing to want and that's what I want. See?"

Fotheringay's face has darkened and become much more forcible.

"I'm about beginning to get the hang of this miracle business. You've all had your say. The only chap who's got near to common horse-sense about it is Bill Stoker—and that won't do *him* much good by the time I've done with him. Come along, Maydig. I may want you. We're going to start the world of George McWhirter Fotheringay right 'ere in the Colonel's house."

---

all that's small beer." Healing and doing good for others is not as important as fulfilling self interest: advice that at last trumps Mr. Maydig's.

39. Director General, or perhaps *dei gratia* (by the grace of God), although Mr. Fotheringay surely knows no Latin. The latter meaning must be the author's ironic commentary on his divine power used for base motives, now fully asserted.

Group receding towards the village. Fotheringay leads, dictatorially musing. Maydig walks at his elbow. He is engaged in silent colloquy with himself and occasionally shakes his head. The Colonel follows sullenly with his useless gun some paces behind.

Ominous music.

Half-length of Fotheringay *en face* brooding, thinking in the rhythm of the music. With the others following.

PART XVI

THE SOLILOQUY

THE Colonel's bed-room. Manly accessories. Riding-boots and spurs. Regimental officers' photographs. Pistols on night-table. A cheval-glass. The door opens and FOTHERINGAY appears. He speaks to someone unseen (Maydig) outside door. "I want to be alone for a bit 'ere. Shan't be long."

He shuts the door on the outer world.

FOTHERINGAY: "You've got Power, George McWhirter, and you can't run away from Power. Got Power? ... Power's got *you*."

He comes to a pause facing the cheval-glass. His hands are in his pockets. "Blood on my face?"

He feels it.

He begins to grimace in front of the glass, folds his arms like Napoleon; then makes an eloquent gestures, arm out.

FOTHERINGAY: "Let me be a little taller and bigger."

The change is effected. He is standing with his back to the audience and the mirror shows his face. It and the room become relatively about one-fifth smaller than before.

FOTHERINGAY: "If I had a higher forehead and a harder mouth—. Let me have a high forehead and a harder mouth.

"Stronger eyes and dark eyebrows."

The mirror shows these changes.

FOTHERINGAY: "Straighter nose and a good moustache."

Long scrutiny of his reflection. "You look a queer chap now. But you aren't me. I don't like you somehow. No, let me be just as I was before I began changing. It's a queer thing, George McWhirter Fotheringay, seeing what a mug you are and what a mug you look, that you don't reely want to be anybody but George McWhirter Fotheringay. You just want to be yourself—until something wipes you out.

"I wonder did anyone *ever* want to be anyone but himself?"

He turns away from the mirror and interrogates himself earnestly. "What do I really want? I can have all the wishes in the world. What do I really want?

"Do I want Ada? I do. And *what* do I want of her? I want her to see I'm Master of the World, I want her to *feel* I'm master and show it—and when she's got that—do I want her any more? Not a bit of it. And Maggie? Maggie too. Instead of all this persuading me and helping me. I want to be Boss and lord of all things, and so does everyone in his heart. But I, mind you, have Power. When I didn't realise I had it, I sang small. But not now. Oh! the Colonel be blowed, old stick-in-the-mud! and Grigsby, the tradesman, be blowed and Bampfylde be blowed. And Maydig be blowed! Maydig in *particular* be blowed. Tell me what to do, he would. Wise advice! Warnings! Ex-hortations. Who wants all this Progress and Service and doing things for other people, and going without oneself? Humbug! Humbug! They want *their* games and I want *my* game. I'll do things for them perhaps—but they'll have to be grateful to me. So we come down to hard tacks at last—it's Me—me, and *more* of me—and *most* of me—George McWhirter Fotheringay!"[40]

Close-up of his excited and glowing face advancing with an effect of exultant menace towards the audience.

---

40. An unusually reflective soliloquy for such as he, justified by artistic license. Mr. Fotheringay, looking into the full-length cheval-glass, finally resolves to be himself and nothing but himself, hidden feelings and desires to the fore. He will be the Boss now, master/man relationships reversed for him: Master of the World. Everything he personally wishes for will be his. When he says, "Got Power? ... Power's got *you*," the author editorializes: What more can be expected of the common man, ludicrous when empowered.

PART XVII

THE WORLD OF GEORGE MCWHIRTER FOTHERINGAY

SCENE. The hall of the Colonel's house.

Maydig and the Colonel hover restlessly. Their mutual aversion is evident. They do not speak. The Colonel is still perplexed and worried by his gun barrel. He takes down some old pistols and examines them. Their barrels have also become solid. Maydig frets up and down, whispers and gesticulates to himself and watches the door through which Fotheringay must come. To them enter BAMPFYLDE who asks: "Has anything more happened?"

COLONEL: "My God! What *hasn't* happened? He's mad and dangerous, and bullets won't kill him."

The study door at the end of the hall opens and Fotheringay appears. His face is deadly white and lit up with excitement.

He approaches the three slowly with a certain air of menace. They do not move; they are in a state of great tension; they wait for him to speak first.

FOTHERINGAY: "I've got my own Ideas at last. This old world of yours—it's over. There's going to be a New Miraculous World. And it's going to be *Mine!*"

BAMPFYLDE: "You have the Power, sir—but—"

FOTHERINGAY: "Any objection?"

BAMPFYLDE: "Changes—even miraculous changes—can be too violent. There is such a thing as inertia."

FOTHERINGAY: "And what's this—*Inertia?*"[41]

---

41. In physics "inertia" is that property of matter by virtue of which it retains its state of rest or of uniform rectilinear motion unless acted on by external force. Hence, by analogy, the force of social tradition having no inherent power of action, the conservative Mr. Bampfylde's usage. He says that to resist social inertia is to invite violence, and for that he is made out to be a reactionary old fool. Fotheringay ignores his advice to go slow, and cosmic disastser results. Yet Wells himself is for a violent "War with Tradition" (1931a:69), the story of *Things to Come*: a fight to combat human nature's "congenital traditionalism" (1932:137). Mr. Fotheringay, however powerful, is not the man to fight that war. It entails "two fundamental opposites in human affairs as we know them — cre-

BAMPFYLDE: "It's a tendency in things to go on as they have been going. You can't even stop a motor-car *dead*."

FOTHERINGAY with a slight grin: "Not without a miracle."

BAMPFYLDE: "You may think I am being needlessly obstructive, but people have to adapt themselves. You have to give them time. Hasten slowly. Advance circumspectly."

FOTHERINGAY: "And never get anything else done! No. We begin 'ere and now. The world of George McWhirter Fotheringay. According to his dreams. According to what he's been told and found out since he began to think about things."

MAYDIG: "One word, sir. Whatever you may think of Mr. Bampfylde, you will at least admit that *I* am not unprogressive. I ask you—before you do anything else—Make a Plan. Nothing can be done without a Plan."

FOTHERINGAY screws his face up: "*What* Plan?"

MAYDIG: "Balance. Order. Creative aims."

FOTHERINGAY: "Plan! Talk away an age! Hesitate! Sway to and fro! Mess about! ... I want my new world now. I want it to come in my lifetime. While I can see it and glory in it and have some fun in it."

BAMPFYLDE: "Wait. Let things go on—just for a little while longer."

FOTHERINGAY smiles contemptuously at him: "'Ere, let this house be changed to a great splendid beautiful palace and us in the great Hall of it. *Now*."

Masterful sweep of the arm.

The four men remain grouped and the wainscotted narrow hall about them dissolves into a gigantic and beautiful interior. To the right are great windows lit up by the rays of the sun, sinking in the west. All that follows is to be grandiose and free from any trace of burlesque. The building can be something after the style of the Stockholm Town Hall. Or better, it can recall Paul Veronese.

FOTHERINGAY: "Not bad, eh? Architecture improving. But we hardly seem dressed for it. 'Ere, let us all be sumptuously dressed according

---

ation and tradition ... a conflict between past claims and future achievement" (1932:20f). Fotheringay, himself a foolish reactionary, harks back to the discredited Boss system of human relations.

In Part XVIII (the Frame again) the Indifference comments on the miracle that stopped the world going round: "everything loose has been flung about by its own inertia." The term is recalled to emphasize that Fotheringay defies not only social inertia but the laws of physics. Later the Indifference in Part XIX says that, despite the Player's faith in human progress, in the end it will be the same old "story of inertia." No. Better men than Fotheringay will work miracles of science that at once will defy tradition and obey the cosmic order of things.

to our characters and stations so as not to look strange here. Me, the Prince, Maydig and Bampfylde like Councillors, the Colonel as the Captain of the Guard. *Now!*"

The change is effected. The costumes can be futuristic—Renaissance—but they must not be extravagant or absurd.

FOTHERINGAY: "You'll like being Captain of the Guard after a bit, Colonel. Looks empty 'ere. What's your regiment, Colonel? Let his old battalion be 'ere and dressed accordingly. Now." (Guards appear.) "And let's have all the butlers and footmen in Essex 'ere as attendants—in suitable clothes. Same style as the building. Sort of rich like. So. Now 'ere's a place I can work in. Room to turn round in. Not bad, is it? You didn't think I liked things Large. You saw to it that I was born small and grew up small. Nobody likes being small.... Let's have a tame panther or two—five *tame* panthers, really tame, mind you—strolling about. I've always had a fancy for panthers. And a couple of elephants wouldn't look bad down there. Let there be two elephants there, all dressed up—driver and all complete." (Miracle gesture.)

FOTHERINGAY: "And now let us have 'ere Miss Ada Price, just as she was yesterday afternoon when I gave her a tiara and made her lovely."

Ada Price appears as Venus-Cleopatra.

FOTHERINGAY: "Well, Ada, my dear, and what do you think of it?"

ADA, surveying the scene: "Why!—there's Colonel Winstanley! All dressed up rich and handsome! This is something *like* a miracle. You're going it, George, at last. Where's *Bill?*"

FOTHERINGAY is stung: "Can't you do without Bill for a moment?"

ADA: "I thought you'd have Bill about—somehow. All this is sort of his style."

FOTHERINGAY controls himself by an effort: "It's *my* style, Ada."

He thinks: "Nothing to sit on? Let there be two thrones here."

They appear.

ADA: "You might have a throne for Bill."

FOTHERINGAY: "No. And that throne isn't for you. Just you stand down there, Ada—that's your place.... Let Maggie Hooper be dressed like a queen and let her come 'ere."

Maggie appears. Maydig, who has been watching events with apprehension, becomes more confident and takes a step nearer.

FOTHERINGAY: "Well, Maggie, 'ere we are beginning the Miraculous Reign of George McWhirter Fotheringay. What shall we do with the world?"

Maggie is too overcome by amazement to speak.

ADA: "Oh! don't make it dull and goody-goody.... George, I didn't mean to say that about Bill! I didn't."

FOTHERINGAY, grimly: "But you said it. No. There's plenty of your sort. You just stand about being lovely—until I take notice of you. And just to keep you company, let the next six prettiest girls in Dewhinton come here—all lovely and beautifully dressed too. Not too much dressed.... My world's going to be full of pretty women, ten a penny."

A group of ladies appears. They appear with an expression of astonishment, look about them and whisper to one another overawed. They become aware of each other's beauty and an overpowering desire to see themselves in mirrors possesses them. One only carries a hand-mirror and this is much in request.

MAGGIE: "Dear George, make the world happy. Don't make it selfish and showy. Let this be really the world's great age."

MAYDIG, still growing in confidence: "Begins anew. Justice. Peace. Plenty."

FOTHERINGAY to Bampfylde: "You think I don't know how to do it. Now you shall see. Nothing in a hurry and nothing delayed. I've learnt a lot these three days—I begin to get the hang of it all."

MAYDIG: "Oh, take thought. Take counsel."

Fotheringay turns to him with a gesture between reassurance and mockery. He intends to take counsel—in his own fashion.

The camera comes round so that Fotheringay stands in half-profile at the head of a great system of staircases with the vast empty space of the palace court before him. Maggie, Ada, Maydig, Bampfylde, the Colonel are grouped about him. Other Councillors appear close to him as the scene proceeds. The camera comes up to his dark profile, beyond which the wide brightly-lit hall is shown.

FOTHERINGAY: "'Ere. Let this Hall stretch so as to be big enough to hold all the people I am going to have 'ere. Let two hundred of the greatest bankers come 'ere and stand 'ere." (A number of rather amazed gentlemen appear.) "There you are. Let the thousand leading men who direct and own great businesses, stand 'ere." (The floor begins to be crowded.) "Let the chief men who rule people, the kings and presidents and politicians and commissars, the men who tell the newspapers what to say, the people who teach and preach. Let them come—yes—five thousand of them. *Now.*"

The Hall far below is rapidly filled with a great multitude of men (and a few women) mostly middle-aged and respectable-looking people. A few priests in robes, a few uniforms are among them. Indian leaders, Chinese generals. Japanese, old style and new. It is *Who's Who*; it is *Who's Who in America*; it is *Europa* and the *Statesman's Year Book* assembled. They have the habitual self-control of men and women accustomed to be seen in public and watched by crowds. They stroll about in a slightly dazed way, accost one another, ask questions and gradually become aware of Fotheringay. The camera can wander over their upturned faces and show a selection of the intellectual life of humanity, in very slight caricature, all looking up at last to Mr. George McWhirter Fotheringay.

FOTHERINGAY: "Now 'ere we are for a great big talk together. I'm just anybody and you are the people who run the world. I've been told to take thought—take council. So I've got you to come 'ere! All of you! Why not?"

He pauses a little out of breath. Goes on with a certain strain in his voice. "Now I've got you. Now I've got the lot of you. All you what have your faces in the papers and sit in high places and walk through crowds of people and get all the cheers and praise! I've got you people who run the world '*ere*, to tell you to run it better. See—" His voice rises in excitement—"RUN IT BETTER."

Close-up of faces of representative prominent men at this announcement.

FOTHERINGAY pauses and then begins to scold: "You're the people who've lived on the fat of the world. You've been *trusted* with the world. Chaps like me have had to trust you, willy-nilly. And what sort of deal did you give us? What did you do for us, for all the trust we gave you? Science made miracles, if I didn't. There was plenty and more than plenty. The papers said so. The professors said so. *You* could go anywhere and do anything. And what did you do for *us*? What was *our* share?"

Protesting faces and cries from statesmen and journalists. An inaudible economist makes explanatory gestures.

"Oh, I know. I had to wait. Wait. Wait. Wait young and seedy—until I get old and seedy. And did. Be patient for umpty years while you held all the stuff in your hands—and did nothing. Much your crowd cared. Did you worry about it? Not a bit. But *you'd better worry now*."

Close-up of indignant group. Uniformed soldier with his hand on revolver.

FOTHERINGAY's finger points to him: "No good shooting at me. I've *been* shot at. It won't work any more. There's an end to shooting. You can't shoot the truth. I'm 'ere and I've come to stay. George McWhirter Fotheringay! Power's gone out of your hands. You can strut about for a bit more and try to look important and play the old tricks, but I tell you Power has gone out of your hands." (Points to the sunset outside the great windows.) "That is *your* sun setting. It's late afternoon for the whole crowd of you. You know it. Gaw!—You try to make an excuse for it. Where has it gone, this Power? It's come to *me*, a common vulgar fellow, and it's driven me wild; it's come to me by a miracle."

Shots of the crowd in unison very intent. Then back to Fotheringay's profile and his gesticulating hand.

"And now you've go to do something, and do it soon. Make a new world that will make me happy. Get together, you Important People down there, and try to *be* reely important for once. Talk it over with each other and talk real stuff. Do it quickly and do it now. What was that trouble you got into about property? Why is property a curse to nearly everybody instead of what you pretend it is, something to ginger us up for our common good? I had none. I don't understand property. But you *know* about it. Did most of you grab too much of it and use it wrong? Did you ever try to clear that up and put it right? And what went wrong with our money? *You* fiddled about with it. Well, if you didn't, you let a lot of rascals fiddle about with it. You stood in. You played little games against each other. Great fun for you. Money! What Mr. Bampfylde calls the life-blood of society—and did you keep it clean? Did you use all the leisure and advantages you had to make it work better? Not you. And why could you never stop war? You could have stopped war. Why, a hundred resolute men in high places who weren't afraid of a bit of brain work, could have stopped war for ever—any time in the last twenty years. But I guess you liked the bands and the spurs and the feathers too much. And you didn't think about chaps like me. Nice and pompous you looked, inspecting the troops—being saluted. And did you really forget about chaps like me? Not even that. Not even that much excuse. A few trenches full of dead chaps like me?[42] *That* made you feel more real and important, eh?"

---

42. Alludes to the dreadful carnage of World War I, 1914–1918. In the midst of it Wells did a hard-hitting pamphlet, *The Peace of the World* (1915a). Mr. Fotheringay mouths the same pieties about world peace with equal force, but he totally misprizes whatever qualities of Wellsian statesmanship are required to achieve it.

According to Wells, contrary to historical experience, it is the modern democratic nation-states that cause international warfare, brought to a new level of destructiveness by mechanical means. In *Things to Come* John Cabal says, "If we don't end war, war will end us." This is to say, If we don't end democracy, democracy will end us.

Wells's logic behind this is plain enough. He believed the ignorant masses, empowered by universal suffrage, *voted* for war out of belligerent patriotism. The Patriot Chief of Everytown in *Things to Come* is wildly cheered after each

Pause with his lips shut, nodding his point home.

Camera picks out an assortment of generals and military men, a foreign minister or so, munition dealers wearing orders, etc. They interrogate one another mutely. Camera returns to Fotheringay.

FOTHERINGAY: "Well now—just clear it all up—*now*. See? While I wait. 'Ere and now. You shan't eat or drink, you shan't leave this place until you've cleared up the muddle you've lived in and kept me in ever since I was born. That's what I've got to say to you. And if you don't do what I tell you, I'll wipe you all out—as a child wipes a slate. That's me. That's what I've found inside me since I began looking. That's what I've dug out of George McWhirter Fotheringay."

MAYDIG to Bampfylde: "He's gone completely mad!"

BAMPFYLDE to Fotheringay: "But they *must* have time to think about it."

FOTHERINGAY: "If I give them time, they'll waste it. They've had—*generations* of time. Their sort. What have they done? What were they doing when I called them 'ere?"

BAMPFYLDE: "But these things cannot be done instantly."

FOTHERINGAY: "They are going to be done—'ere and now. A good and happy world. A sensible world. Then, when I've got that off my chest, we'll see." (He glances with a sort of affectionate desire at the ladies in waiting.) "We'll see about what can be made of living."

---

victory over neighboring ministates: decivilized remnants of a second world war. Although the Boss, Rudolph the Victorious, caricatures Mussolini and Hitler, the dishonest suggestion is that these popular European dictators are examples of a species of totalitarian democracy. So, one way or the other, democracy is the cause of war. John Cabal the great Air Dictator, after extinguishing the likes of Rudolph, imposes the real thing in dictatorship.

Miracles was published in 1936, the year in which a five-power disarmament treaty ran out. Signed at the Washington Conference of 1921 convened by U.S. President Warren G. Harding, Wells covered the story in a series of newspaper articles, collected in *Washington and the Hope of Peace* (1922).

The first article is titled "The Immensity of the Issue and the Triviality of Men" (1922:1), the issue being world peace. So imperative is it that, unless war and nationalism are ended, the world may smash itself beyond recovery. Compared to the catastrophic greatness of that possible event, the lives of individual men are indeed trivial: the essential point of Wells's cosmic vision.

Mr. Fotheringay with his last miracle wrecks the world, equivalent to a great war catastrophe. The impersonal Airmen salvage what is left of civilization and begin a unified world-state. They save mankind from its collective democratic stupidity, concentrated in Mr. Fotheringay's demagogic speech in Part XVII.

BAMPFYLDE, trying to reason with himself as well as Fotheringay: "There is an inertia in things that drives us on."

FOTHERINGAY: "Inertia!—I'm always up against this inertia. There is a power in *me* that wants a change. I'm sick of your old world and its Inertia!"

MAYDIG: "But at least wait until to-morrow. The sun is setting. Give them the night to think and discuss."

FOTHERINGAY: "No hurry about the sunset. I can stop that sunset. I want my new world now."

A NEW COUNCILLOR close at hand speaks.

"You can't stop the sun in the sky, sir!"

FOTHERINGAY: "*What!* I tell you I can."

The NEW COUNCILLOR: "No sir. All the planets will fly off into outer space and outer darkness."

FOTHERINGAY: "One might think you were a banker, to hear you talk."

The NEW COUNCILLOR: "I'm a professor of physics."

FOTHERINGAY: "Well, *I'll* stop the sun setting. I won't *have* it set. Not till I want to go to bed—after we've cleared things up."

The NEW COUNCILLOR: "But then you'd have to stop the earth rotating!"

FOTHERINGAY: "And I WILL. No, don't argue with me, Maydig, don't argue with me, anyone. There's a time when argument stops."

He clenches his fists and stamps his foot. He becomes frantic with passion.

"'Ere, Earth, stop rotating *now!* *Now!* Stop."[43]

The music, which has been increasingly uneasy, rises to an immense thud, which leaves everything throbbing. Everything flies off into streaks. The vibrations change into a torrent of sound which returns into the grandiose motifs of the opening Sequence.

---

43. The professor of physics dares to tell Mr. Fotheringay that, in effect, his pre–Copernican view of the solar system is long outdated: the sun only *appears* to rise and set, when it is the earth's movement around the sun that creates that illusion. Very well, Mr. Fotheringay will not attempt the impossible miracle reported in Joshua 10:12, "Sun, stand thou still." Instead, he commands the earth to stop rotating on its axis. Instantly, as predicted, a catastrophic storm begins.

PART XVIII

THE LAST MOMENT

THE starry universe. The there great Spirits of the opening Sequence appear against the stars.

The Player sits and looks down at the earth. The two others look over his shoulder.

The undertow of music becomes more manifest, it rises gradually to a powerful throbbing.

The PLAYER: "What has happened?"

The OBSERVER: "He's stopped the world going round!"

The INDIFFERENCE: "Not—suddenly?"

The OBSERVER: "Yes."

The INDIFFERENCE: "Then everything loose has been flung about by its own inertia—and that is the end of your nasty little pets upon their silly little planet. Preposterous! What did I tell you? It's all over. Come."

PLAYER: "No, no. It's not over. *He's* still alive—he's got a charmed life. He saw to that."

The OBSERVER, bending down closer: "Hit! No. Miss! He's missed again. *That* nearly had him. He's certainly got a charmed life."

Transition effects: a moment of 'abstract film.' It slows down and resolves itself into a rush of concrete objects. The music now throbs and beats and storms at the ears of the audience. A torrent, a Niagara rush of flying objects sweeps across the screen, trees, buildings, machinery, ships, water, railway-bridges, mountain-masses, the world flung headlong through the air. The atmosphere also is wildly disturbed. Screaming gale. Torn clouds streaming out and vast glares and forks of lightning. Wild torrents of whooping music also. Crashes and crescendos.

Fotheringay is seen flying head over heels, head over heels, in this tornado of objects. He goes in loping jerks. The elephant from his court nearly hits him. A large obelisk misses him by a yard. The voice of the OBSERVER is heard remotely: "Hit! No! Miss."

FOTHERINGAY's voice comes in jerks: "Let everything be. As it was—a minute before—I went into the Long Dragon."

Momentarily swift arrest of things flying in the air. They must all swing round like ships coming about, and then stream down into a rush of black and grey lines which immediately swirl about and become the opening village scene of Sequence II. It is the street outside the Long Dragon. Fotheringay is seen outside the inn door.

He stands scratching his head. He looks up at the sky. Was it a dream?

"Hold hard for a bit. We haven't done yet. These miracles! If it happens that I *have* been working miracles, at the word Go, let me not be able to work any more miracles ever. No more miracles. And forget all about it. Forget about it. Wipe it out. You can't control it. *Go!*"

The pillar of vibrating ebon darkness which endowed him with his gift, appears above his head, quivers in black splendour and passes up into the sky.

PART XIX

THE MIGHTY POWERS MAKE THEIR COMMENTS

RETURN again to the three great Spirits of the opening Sequence.

The INDIFFERENCE: "So he wouldn't have your gift. He threw it back to you."

The OBSERVER: "But he destroyed his world first. Your silly little planet has had a narrow squeak, Brother. Look at them. Not a soul among them realises that a minute ago every one of them was hurled headlong and smashed to pieces and brought back to life by a miracle."

The INDIFFERENCE: "They know nothing. He said 'Forget it.' And what has your experiment shown, Brother? What did you get out of that sample man? Egotism and elementary lust. A little vindictive indignation. That's all the creatures have—or will have for ever. What can you make of them?"

The PLAYER: "They were apes only yesterday. Give them time."[44]

The INDIFFERENCE: "Once an ape—always an ape."

The PLAYER: "You say they are all just egotism and lust. No. There was something in every one of those creatures more than that. Like a little grain of gold glittering in sand, lost in the sand. A flash of indignation when they think things are false and wrong. That's God-like. Dirt is never indignant. That's why they interest me."

The OBSERVER: "Their indignation is always selfish. They are in a mess. They were made by the mess. They are made for the mess. They are part of the mess. They will never get out of their mess."

The PLAYER: "But if I give them power, not suddenly but bit by bit. If I stir thought and wisdom into the mess to keep pace with the growth of power. Broaden slowly. Age by age. Give the grains of gold time to get together."[45]

---

44. In the vast scheme of geological time, man's apelike origins were indeed "only yesterday." Progress in future is indicated.

45. The Player here sums up the film story's Wellsian thesis. In time those "little grains of gold" scattered in the sand of human dross will get together, as

The INDIFFERENCE: "And in the end it will be the same. A story of inertia, a story long drawn out instead of swift and sudden. But petty to the end."
The PLAYER: "No. It will be different."
The INDIFFERENCE, incredulous: "You say No? Still you say No!"
The PLAYER: "Come back here in an age or so and you shall see...."

---

they do in *Things to Come*. John Cabal's Airmen, gathered from both sides of World War II, get together and recognize each other for what they are, commencing the unitary world state under grandson Oswald Cabal. Wells is elsewhere unfashionably candid in defining the problem. "The average contemporary man *en masse* is definitely a degenerate creature." Destined to govern them are "exceptional types," an "emergent elite" (1944:192) — those "grains of gold" in *Miracles*.

In the 1936 screen version of *Things to Come*, realizing a sequence in the 1935 film story, how this emergent elite will go about its business is most tellingly shot in almost complete silence. The Airmen are loading up one of their bombers for a raid on Everytown; they will drop the Gas of Peace on it, then parachute in to take over. Some Airmen place boxes of bombs onto a rail leading into the plane while others, parachutes on their backs, enter it through a doorway after smartly going up a pair of steps. Inside, others pack the bombs (glass globes with the Gas of Peace) in place by the bombardier's station. Two men outside take the rail away, others remove the steps, and yet another shuts the door.

Everyone knows his function with machine-like coordination, no bossing on the spot. They all do their duty with speechless precision, on their way to wipe out Rudolph, the loud-mouthed Boss of Everytown. In the event, the Gas of Peace (a pacifying nerve agent) kills only *him*; the rest awaken and a new world begins. The degenerate masses are regenerated for their proper place in different schemes of things. John Cabal "the great Air Dictator," as he is called, is not unlike Plato's philosopher king. He lays down a philosophy of social efficiency derived from the production factory, wherein its division of labor is coordinated from a managerial center. The functional object is industrial productivity, not bossing along feudalistic master-man lines.

PART XX

DA CAPO

THE scene returns to the bar-parlour of the Long Dragon at Dewhinton. At first it is, as it were, transparent. For some moments, that is, the constellations shine through the scene and fade slowly and vanish imperceptibly. The characters are the same and posed in the same attitudes as they were at the point in Sequence II when FOTHERINGAY says: "A miracle, *I* say, is something *contrariwise* to the usual course of nature, done by power of will—something that couldn't happen, not without being specially willed."

TODDY BEAMISH: "So *you* say."

FOTHERINGAY: "Well, you got to 'ave a definition." (Appeals to cyclist.) "What do *you* say, sir?"

Cyclist starts, clears his throat and expresses assent.

Fotheringay appeals to Landlord Cox.

COX: "I'm not *in* this."

TODDY BEAMISH: "Well, I agree. Contrariwise to the usual course of nature. 'Ave it so. And what about it?"

FOTHERINGAY, pursuing his argument: "For instance. 'Ere would be a miracle. The lamp 'ere, in the natural course of nature, couldn't burn like that upsy-down, could it, Mr. Beamish?"

TODDY BEAMISH: "*You* say it couldn't."

FOTHERINGAY: "And you? Wah!—you don't mean to say—No?"

TODDY BEAMISH: "No. Well. It couldn't."

FOTHERINGAY: "Very well. Then 'ere comes someone, as it might be me, along 'ere, and he stands as it might be 'ere, and he says to this lamp, as I might do, collecting all my will—and I'm doing it mind you—I'm playing fair: 'Turn upsy-down, I tell you, without breaking and go on burning steady.'" (Pause.) "Well, there, you see, nothing happens!"

COX: "Nothing *could* happen like that. It wouldn't be sense."

FOTHERINGAY: "Exactly. And miracles aren't sense."

MISS MAYBRIDGE, busy wiping out her beer-glasses: "All the same, I sometimes wish *I* could work miracles."

FOTHERINGAY, lounging: "I wonder what you'd *do* if you could work miracles."

MISS MAYBRIDGE: "Oh—I'd do lots of nice things." (Slight pause.)

TODDY BEAMISH: "I'd make the world a better place. Within reason." They all follow their own train of thought for a second or so.

FOTHERINGAY becomes thoughtful; he makes the miracle gesture, but nothing ensues. "There's one or two things I'd like to do."

TODDY BEAMISH: "But you won't ever have the chance."

FOTHERINGAY, leaning half back to the bar and nodding his head a little ruefully. "No, I won't ever have the chance—Na-ow."[46]

Close-up of his face—as though some phantom memory eluded him. "Na-ow." He lifts his hand and drops it again. Music swells, begins the miracle motif once more, loses heart and dies down to a sigh. Fade out slowly.

THE END

---

46. The film story concludes with Mr. Fotheringay wistfully reflecting that "na-ow" (lower class cockney accent) he no longer has the power to work miracles. Of course he cannot possibly remember that he ever had it. He merely muses on a power fantasy impossible for the common little man to realize. The real drift of events, as given in *Things to Come*, go against empowerment for such as he when massed for voting in a democracy.

The concluding Part XX to *Miracles*, "Da Capo," comes from the Italian musical term, to repeat from the beginning. Mr. Fotheringay in the Long Dragon repeats his predigestary gesture, but the lamp does *not* turn upside down. That is the way it has to be in Wellsian terms. The masses may as well vote against the law of gravity as for their own selfish class interest, with upsetting results for all humanity.

Appendix I
"The Man Who Could Work Miracles," by H.G. Wells (1898)

Here is the short story Wells drew upon for his film story offered in the present volume. It first appeared, before reprinting in 1927a, in the July 1898 issue of *The London Illustrated News*. In those days, newspapers were more than newspapers as we know them today. They most often published anything but news, richly illustrated, including fiction.

The 1936 film story has its essentials there, but with a notable difference. The Frame brings in Wells's passion to convey a sense of cosmic vision. The story's cute subtitle, "A Pantoum [pantun] in Prose," alludes to a supposedly Malayan verse form in which the last stanza repeats the first: the *"Da Capo"* of the film story's final Part XX.

THE MAN WHO COULD WORK MIRACLES

A Pantoum in Prose

IT IS doubtful whether the gift was innate. For my own part, I think it came to him suddenly. Indeed, until he was thirty he was a sceptic, and did not believe in miraculous powers. And here, since it is the most convenient place, I must mention that he was a little man, and had eyes of a hot brown, very erect red hair, a moustache with ends that he twisted up, and freckles. His name was George McWhirter Fotheringay—not the sort of name by any means to lead to any expectation of miracles—and he was clerk at Gomshott's. He was greatly addicted to assertive argument. It was while he was asserting the impossibility of miracles that he had his first intimation of his extraordinary powers. This particular argument was being held in the bar of the Long

Dragon, and Toddy Beamish was conducting the opposition by a monotonous but effective "So *you* say," that drove Mr. Fotheringay to the very limit of his patience.

There were present, besides these two, a very dusty cyclist, landlord Cox, and Miss Maybridge, the perfectly respectable and rather portly barmaid of the Dragon. Miss Maybridge was standing with her back to Mr. Fotheringay, washing glasses; the others were watching him, more or less amused by the present ineffectiveness of the assertive method. Goaded by the Torres Vedras tactics of Mr. Beamish, Mr. Fotheringay determined to make an unusual rhetorical effort. "Looky here, Mr. Beamish," said Mr. Fotheringay. "Let us clearly understand what a miracle is. It's something contrariwise to the course of nature done by power of Will, something what couldn't happen without being specially willed."

"So *you* say," said Mr. Beamish, repulsing him.

Mr. Fotheringay appealed to the cyclist, who had hitherto been a silent auditor, and received his assent—given with a hesitating cough and a glance at Mr. Beamish. The landlord would express no opinion, and Mr. Fotheringay, returning to Mr. Beamish, received the unexpected concession of a qualified assent to his definition of a miracle.

"For instance," said Mr. Fotheringay, greatly encouraged. "Here would be a miracle. That lamp, in the natural course of nature, couldn't burn like that upsy-down, could it, Beamish?"

"*You* say it couldn't," said Beamish.

"And you?" said Fotheringay. "You don't mean to say—eh?"

"No," said Beamish reluctantly. "No, it couldn't."

"Very well," said Mr. Fotheringay. "Then here comes someone, as it might be me, along here, and stands as it might be here, and says to that lamp, as I might do, collecting all my will—'Turn upsy-down without breaking, and go on burning steady,' and—— Hullo!"

It was enough to make anyone say "Hullo!" The impossible, the incredible, was visible to them all. The lamp hung inverted in the air, burning quietly with its flame pointing down. It was as solid, as indisputable as ever a lamp was, the prosaic common lamp of the Long Dragon bar.

Mr. Fotheringay stood with an extended forefinger and the knitted brows of one anticipating a catastrophic smash. The cyclist, who was sitting next the lamp, ducked and jumped across the bar. Everybody jumped, more or less. Miss Maybridge turned and screamed. For nearly three seconds the lamp remained still. A faint cry of mental distress came from Mr. Fotheringay. "I can't keep it up," he said, "any longer." He staggered back, and the inverted lamp suddenly flared, fell against the corner of the bar, bounced aside, smashed upon the floor, and went out.

It was lucky it had a metal receiver, or the whole place would have been in a blaze. Mr. Cox was the first to speak, and his remark, shorn of needless excrescences, was to the effect that Fotheringay was a fool. Fotheringay was beyond disputing even so fundamental a proposition as that! He was astonished beyond measure at the thing that had occurred. The subsequent conversation threw absolutely no light on the matter so far as Fotheringay was concerned; the general opinion not only followed Mr. Cox very closely but very vehemently. Everyone accused Fotheringay of a silly trick, and presented him to himself as a foolish destroyer of comfort and security. His mind was in a tornado of perplexity, he was himself inclined to agree with them, and he made a remarkably ineffectual opposition to the proposal of his departure.

He went home flushed and heated, coat-collar crumpled, eyes smarting, and ears red. He watched each of the ten street lamps nervously as he passed it. It was only when he found himself alone in his little bedroom in Church Row that he was able to grapple seriously with his memories of the occurrence, and ask, "What on earth happened?"

He had removed his coat and boots, and was sitting on the bed with his hands in his pockets repeating the text of his defence for the seventeenth time, "*I* didn't want the confounded thing to upset," when it occurred to him that at the precise moment he had said the commanding words he had inadvertently willed the thing he said, and that when he had seen the lamp in the air he had felt that it depended on him to maintain it there without being clear how this was to be done. He had not a particularly complex mind, or he might have stuck for a time at that "inadvertently willed," embracing, as it does, the abstrusest problems of voluntary action; but as it was, the idea came to him with a quite acceptable haziness. And from that, following, as I must admit, no clear logical path, he came to the test of experiment.

He pointed resolutely to his candle and collected his mind, though he felt he did a foolish thing. "Be raised up," he said. But in a second that feeling vanished. The candle was raised, hung in the air one giddy moment, and as Mr. Fotheringay gasped, fell with a smash on his toilet-table, leaving him in darkness save for the expiring glow of its wick.

For a time Mr. Fotheringay sat in the darkness, perfectly still. "It did happen, after all," he said. "And 'ow I'm to explain it I *don't* know." He sighed heavily, and began feeling in his pockets for a match. He could find none, and he rose and groped about the toilet-table. "I wish

I had a match," he said. He resorted to his coat, and there were none there, and then it dawned upon him that miracles were possible even with matches. He extended a hand and scowled at it in the dark. "Let there be a match in that hand," he said. He felt some light object fall across his palm, and his fingers closed upon a match.

After several ineffectual attempts to light this, he discovered it was a safety-match. He threw it down, and then it occurred to him that he might have willed it lit. He did, and perceived it burning in the midst of his toilet-table mat. He caught it up hastily, and it went out. His perception of possibilities enlarged, and he felt for and replaced the candle in its candlestick. "Here! *you* be lit," said Mr. Fotheringay, and forthwith the candle was flaring, and he saw a little black hole in the toilet-cover, with a wisp of smoke rising from it. For a time he stared from this to the little flame and back, and then looked up and met his own gaze in the looking-glass. By this help he communed with himself in silence for a time.

"How about miracles now?" said Mr. Fotheringay at last, addressing his reflection.

The subsequent meditations of Mr. Fotheringay were of a severe but confused description. So far as he could see, it was a case of pure willing with him. The nature of his first experiences disinclined him for any further experiments except of the most cautious type. But he lifted a sheet of paper, and turned a glass of water pink and then green, and he created a snail, which he miraculously annihilated, and got himself a miraculous new toothbrush. Somewhen in the small hours he had reached the fact that his will-power must be of a particularly rare and pungent quality, a fact of which he had certainly had inklings before, but no certain assurance. The scare and perplexity of his first discovery were now qualified by pride in this evidence of singularity and by vague intimations of advantage. He became aware that the church clock was striking one, and as it did not occur to him that his daily duties at Gomshott's might be miraculously dispensed with, he resumed undressing, in order to get to bed without further delay. As he struggled to get his shirt over his head he was struck with a brilliant idea. "Let me be in bed," he said, and found himself so. "Undressed," he stipulated; and, finding the sheets cold, added hastily, "and in my nightshirt—no, in a nice soft woollen nightshirt. Ah!" he said with immense enjoyment. "And now let me be comfortable asleep...."

He awoke at his usual hour and was pensive all through breakfast-time, wondering whether his overnight experience might not be a particularly vivid dream. At length his mind turned again to cautious experiments. For instance, he had three eggs for breakfast; two his landlady had supplied, good, but shoppy, and one was a delicious fresh goose-egg, laid, cooked, and served by his extraordinary will. He hurried off to Gomshott's in a state of profound but carefully concealed excitement, and only remembered the shell of the third egg when his landlady spoke of it that night. All day he could do no work because of this astonishingly new self-knowledge, but this caused him no inconvenience, because he made up for it miraculously in his last ten minutes.

As the day wore on his state of mind passed from wonder to elation, albeit the circumstances of his dismissal from the Long Dragon were still disagreeable to recall, and a garbled account of the matter that had reached his colleagues led to some badinage. It was evident he must be careful how he lifted frangible articles, but in other ways his gift promised more and more as he turned it over in his mind. He intended among other things to increase his personal property by unostentatious acts of creation. He called into existence a pair of very splendid diamond studs, and hastily annihilated them again as young Gomshott came cross the counting-house to his desk. He was afraid young Gomshott might wonder how he had come by them. He saw quite clearly the gift required caution and watchfulness in its exercise, but so far as he could judge the difficulties attending its mastery would be no greater than those he had already faced in the study of cycling. It was that analogy, perhaps, quite as much as the feeling that he would be unwelcome in the Long Dragon, that drove him out after supper into the lane beyond the gas-works, to rehearse a few miracles in private.

There was possibly a certain want of originality in his attempts, for apart from his will-power Mr. Fotheringay was not a very exceptional man. The miracle of Moses' rod came to his mind, but the night was dark and unfavourable to the proper control of large miraculous snakes. Then he recollected the story of "Tannhäuser" that he had read on the back of the Philharmonic programme. That seemed to him singularly attractive and harmless. He stuck his walking-stick—a very nice Poona-Penang lawyer—into the turf that edged the footpath, and commanded the dry wood to blossom. The air was immediately full of the scent of roses, and by means of a match he saw for himself that this beautiful miracle was indeed accomplished. His satisfaction was ended by advancing footsteps. Afraid of a premature discovery of his powers, he addressed the blossoming stick hastily: "Go back." What he meant was "Change back"; but of course he was confused. The stick receded at a considerable velocity, and incontinently came a cry of anger and a bad word from the approaching person. "Who are you throwing brambles at, you fool?" cried a voice. "That got me on the shin."

"I'm sorry, old chap," said Mr. Fotheringay, and then, realising the awkward nature of the explanation, caught nervously at his moustache. He saw Winch, one of the three Immering constables, advancing.

"What d'yer mean by it?" asked the constable. "Hullo! It's you, is it? The gent that broke the lamp at the Long Dragon!"

"I don't mean anything by it," said Mr. Fotheringay. "Nothing at all."

"What d'yer do it for then?"

"Oh, bother!" said Mr. Fotheringay.

"Bother, indeed? D'yer know that stick hurt? What d'yer do it for, eh?"

For the moment Mr. Fotheringay could not think what he had done it for. His silence seemed to irritate Mr. Winch. "You've been assaulting the police, young man, this time. That's what *you* done."

"Look here, Mr. Winch," said Mr. Fotheringay, annoyed and confused, "I'm very sorry. The fact is——"

"Well?"

He could think of no way but the truth. "I was working a miracle." He tried to speak in an off-hand way, but try as he would he couldn't.

"Working a——! 'Ere, don't you talk rot. Working a miracle, indeed! Miracle! Well, that's downright funny! Why, you's the chap that don't believe in miracles.... Fact is, this is another of your silly conjuring tricks—that's what this is. Now, I tell you——"

But Mr. Fotheringay never heard what Mr. Winch was going to tell him. He realised that he had given himself away, flung his valuable secret to all the winds of heaven. A violent gust of irritation swept him to action. He turned on the constable swiftly and fiercely. "Here," he said, "I've had enough of this, I have! I'll show you a silly conjuring trick, I will! Go to Hades! Go, now!"

He was alone!

Mr. Fotheringay performed no more miracles that night nor did he trouble to see what had become of his flowering stick. He returned to the town, scared and very quiet, and went to his bedroom. "Lord!" he said, "it's a powerful gift—an extremely powerful gift. I didn't hardly mean as much as that. Not really.... I wonder what Hades is like!"

He sat on the bed taking off his boots. Struck by a happy thought he transferred the constable to San Francisco, and without any more interference with normal causation went soberly to bed. In the night he dreamt of the anger of Winch.

The next day Mr. Fotheringay heard two interesting items of news. Someone had planted a most beautiful climbing rose against the elder Mr. Gomshott's private house in the Lullaborough Road, and the river as far as Rawling's Mill was to be dragged for Constable Winch.

Mr. Fotheringay was abstracted and thoughtful all that day, and performed no miracles except certain provisions for Winch, and the miracle of completing his day's work with punctual perfection in spite of all the bee-swarms of thoughts that hummed through his mind. And the extraordinary abstraction and meekness of his manner was remarked by several people, and made a matter for jesting. For the most part he was thinking of Winch.

On Sunday evening he went to chapel, and oddly enough, Mr. Maydig, who took a certain interest in occult matters, preached about "things that are not lawful." Mr. Fotheringay was not a regular chapel goer, but the system of assertive scepticism, to which I have already alluded, was now very much shaken. The tenor of the sermon threw an entirely new light on these novel gifts, and he suddenly decided to consult Mr. Maydig immediately after the service. So soon as that was determined, he found himself wondering why he had not done so before.

Mr. Maydig, a lean, excitable man with quite remarkably long wrists and neck, was gratified at a request for a private conversation from a young man whose carelessness in religious matters was a subject for general remark in the town. After a few necessary delays, he conducted him to the study of the Manse, which was contiguous to the chapel, seated him comfortably, and, standing in front of a cheerful fire—his legs threw a Rhodian arch of shadow on the opposite wall—requested Mr. Fotheringay to state his business.

At first Mr. Fotheringay was a little abashed, and found some difficulty in opening the matter. "You will scarcely believe me, Mr. Maydig, I am afraid"—and so forth for some time. He tried a question at last, and asked Mr. Maydig his opinion of miracles.

Mr. Maydig was still saying "Well" in an extremely judicial tone, when Mr. Fotheringay interrupted again: "You don't believe, I suppose, that some common sort of person—like myself, for instance—as it might be sitting here now, might have some sort of twist inside him that made him able to do things by his will."

"It's possible," said Mr. Maydig. "Something of the sort, perhaps, is possible."

"If I might make free with something here, I think I might show you by a sort of experiment," said Mr. Fotheringay. "Now, take that tobacco-jar on the table, for instance. What I want to know is whether what I am going to do with it is a miracle or not. Just half a minute, Mr. Maydig, please."

He knitted his brows, pointed to the tobacco-jar and said: "Be a bowl of vi'lets."

The tobacco-jar did as it was ordered.

Mr. Maydig started violently at the change, and stood looking from the thaumaturgist to the bowl of flowers. He said nothing. Presently he ventured to lean over the table and smell the violets; they were fresh-picked and very fine ones. Then he stared at Mr. Fotheringay again.

"How did you do that?" he asked.

Mr. Fotheringay pulled his moustache. "Just told it—and there you are. Is that a miracle, or is it black art, or what is it? And what do you think's the matter with me? That's what I want to ask."

"It's a most extraordinary occurrence."

"And this day last week I knew no more that I could do things like that than you did. It came quite sudden. It's something odd about my will, I suppose, and that's as far as I can see."

"Is *that*—the only thing? Could you do other things besides that?"

"Lord, yes!" said Mr. Fotheringay. "Just anything." He thought, and suddenly recalled a conjuring entertainment he had seen. "Here!" He pointed. "Change into a bowl of fish—no, not that—change into a glass bowl full of water with goldfish swimming in it. That's better! You see that, Mr. Maydig?"

"It's astonishing. It's incredible. You are either a most extraordinary ... But no——"

"I could change it into anything," said Mr. Fotheringay. "Just anything. Here! be a pigeon, will you?"

In another moment a blue pigeon was fluttering round the room and making Mr. Maydig duck every time it came near him. "Stop there, will you," said Mr. Fotheringay; and the pigeon hung motionless in the air. "I could change it back to a bowl of flowers," he said, and after replacing the pigeon on the table worked that miracle. "I expect you will want your pipe in a bit," he said, and restored the tobacco-jar.

Mr. Maydig had followed all these later changes in a sort of ejaculatory silence. He stared at Mr. Fotheringay and, in a very gingerly manner, picked up the tobacco-jar, examined it, replaced it on the table. "*Well!*" was the only expression of his feelings.

"Now, after that it's easier to explain what I came about," said Mr. Fotheringay; and proceeded to a lengthy and involved narrative of his strange experiences, beginning with the affair of the lamp in the Long Dragon and complicated by persistent allusions to Winch. As he went on, the transient pride Mr. Maydig's consternation had caused passed away; he became the very ordinary Mr. Fotheringay of everyday intercourse again. Mr. Maydig listened intently, the tobacco-jar in his hand, and his bearing changed also with the course of the narrative. Presently, while Mr. Fotheringay was dealing with the miracle of the third egg, the minister interrupted with a fluttering extended hand—

"It is possible," he said. "It is credible. It is amazing, of course, but it reconciles a number of difficulties. The power to work miracles is a gift—a peculiar quality like genius or second sight—hitherto it has come vary rarely and to exceptional people. But in this case ... I have always wondered at the miracles of Mahomet, and at Yogi's miracles, and the miracles of Madame Blavatsky. But, of course! Yes, it is simply a gift! It carries out so beautifully the arguments of that great thinker"—Mr. Maydig's voice sank—"his Grace the Duke of Argyll. Here we plumb some profounder law—deeper than the ordinary laws of nature. Yes—yes. Go on. Go on!"

Mr. Fotheringay proceeded to tell of his misadventure with Winch, and Mr. Maydig, no longer overawed or scared, began to jerk his limbs about and interject astonishment. "It's this what troubled me most," proceeded Mr. Fotheringay; "it's this I'm most mijitly in want of advice for; of course he's at San Francisco—wherever San Francisco might be—but of course it's awkward for both of us, as you'll see, Mr. Maydig. I don't see how he can understand what has happened, and I dare say he's scared and exasperated something tremendous, and trying to get at me. I dare say he keeps on starting off to come here. I send him back, by a miracle, every few hours, when I think of it. And of course, that's a thing he won't be able to understand, and it's bound to annoy him; and, of course, if he takes a ticket every time it will cost him a lot of money. I done the best I could for him, but of course it's difficult for him to put himself in my place. I thought afterwards that his clothes might have got scorched, you know—if Hades is all it's supposed to be—before I shifted him. In that case I suppose they'd have locked him up in San Francisco. Of course I willed him a new suit of clothes on him directly I thought of it. But, you see, I'm already in a deuce of a tangle——"

Mr. Maydig looked serious. "I see you are in a tangle. Yes, it's a difficult position. How you are to end it..." He became diffuse and inconclusive.

"However, we'll leave Winch for a little and discuss a larger question. I don't think this is a case of the black art or anything of the sort. I don't think there is any taint of criminality about it at all, Mr. Fotheringay—none whatever, unless you are suppressing material facts. No, it's miracles—pure miracles—miracles, if I may say so, of the very highest class."

He began to pace the hearthrug and gesticulate, while Mr. Fotheringay sat with his arm on the table and his head on his arm, looking worried. "I don't see how I'm to manage about Winch," he said.

"A gift of working miracles—apparently a very powerful gift," said Mr. Maydig, "will find a way about Winch—never fear. My dear sir, you are a most important man—a man of the most astonishing possibilities. As evidence, for example! And in other ways, the things you may do...."

"Yes, *I've* thought of a thing or two," said Mr. Fotheringay. "But—some of the things came a bit twisty. You saw that fish at first? Wrong sort of bowl and wrong sort of fish. And I thought I'd ask someone."

"A proper course," said Mr. Maydig, "a very proper course—altogether the proper course." He stopped and looked at Mr. Fotheringay. "It's practically an unlimited gift. Let us test your powers, for instance. If they really *are*... If they really are all they seem to be."

And so, incredible as it may seem, in the study of the little house behind the Congregational Chapel, on the evening of Sunday, Nov. 10, 1896, Mr. Fotheringay, egged on and inspired by Mr. Maydig, began to work miracles. The reader's attention is specially and definitely called to the date. He will object, probably has already objected, that certain points in this story are improbable, that if any things of the sort already described had indeed occurred, they would have been in all the papers a year ago. The details immediately following he will find particularly hard to accept, because among other things they involve the conclusion that he or she, the reader in question, must have been killed in a violent and unprecedented manner more than a year ago. Now a miracle is nothing if not improbable, and as a matter of fact the reader *was* killed in a violent and unprecedented manner a year ago. In the subsequent course of this story that will become perfectly clear and credible, as every right-minded and reasonable reader will admit. But this is not the place for the end of the story, being but little beyond the hither side of the middle. And at first the miracles worked by Mr. Fotheringay were timid little miracles—little things with the cups and parlour fitments, as feeble as the miracles of Theosophists, and, feeble as they were, they were received with awe by his collaborator. He would have preferred to settle the Winch business out of hand, but Mr. Maydig would not let him. But after they had worked a dozen of these domestic trivialities, their sense of power grew, their imagination began to show signs of stimulation, and their ambition enlarged. Their first larger enterprise was due to hunger and the negligence of Mrs. Minchin, Mr. Maydig's housekeeper. The meal to which the minister conducted Mr. Fotheringay was certainly ill-laid and uninviting as refreshment for two industrious miracle-workers; but they were seated, and Mr. Maydig was descanting in sorrow rather than in anger upon his housekeeper's shortcomings, before it occurred to Mr. Fotheringay that an opportunity lay before him. "Don't you think, Mr. Maydig," he said, "if it isn't a liberty, I——"

"My dear Mr. Fotheringay! Of course! No—I didn't think."

Mr. Fotheringay waved his hand. "What shall we have?" he said, in a large, inclusive spirit, and, at Mr. Maydig's order, revised the supper very thoroughly. "As for me," he said, eyeing Mr. Maydig's selection, "I am always particularly fond of a tankard of stout and a nice Welsh rarebit, and I'll order that. I ain't much given to Burgundy," and forth with stout and Welsh rarebit promptly appeared at his command. They sat long at their supper, talking like equals, as Mr. Fotheringay presently perceived with a glow of surprise and gratification, of all the miracles they would presently do. "And, by the bye, Mr. Maydig," said Mr. Fotheringay, "I might perhaps be able to help you—in a domestic way."

"Don't quite follow," said Mr. Maydig, pouring out a glass of miraculous old Burgundy.

Mr. Fotheringay helped himself to a second Welsh rarebit out of vacancy, and took a mouthful. "I was thinking," he said, "I might be able (*chum, chum*) to work (*chum, chum*) a miracle with Mrs. Minchin (*chum, chum*)—make her a better woman."

Mr. Maydig put down the glass and looked doubtful. "She's—— She strongly objects to interference, you know, Mr. Fotheringay. And—as a matter of fact—it's well past eleven and she's probably in bed and asleep. Do you think, on the whole——"

Mr. Fotheringay considered these objections. "I don't see that it shouldn't be done in her sleep."

For a time Mr. Maydig opposed the idea, and then he yielded. Mr. Fotheringay issued his orders, and a little less at their ease, perhaps, the two gentlemen proceeded with their repast. Mr. Maydig was enlarging on the changes he might expect in his housekeeper next day, with an optimism that seemed even to Mr. Fotheringay's supper senses a little forced and hectic, when a series of confused noises from upstairs began. Their eyes exchanged interrogations, and Mr. Maydig left the room hastily. Mr. Fotheringay heard him calling up to his housekeeper and then his footsteps going softly up to her.

In a minute or so the minister returned, his step light, his face radiant. "Wonderful!" he said, "and touching! Most touching!"

He began pacing the hearthrug. "A repentance—a most touching repentance—through the crack of the door. Poor woman! A most wonderful change! She had got up. She must have got up at once. She had got up out of her sleep to smash a private bottle of brandy in her box. And to confess it, too! ... But this gives us—it opens—a most amazing vista of possibilities. If we can work this miraculous change in *her*..."

"The thing's unlimited seemingly," said Mr. Fotheringay. "And about Mr. Winch——"

"Altogether unlimited." And from the hearthrug Mr. Maydig, waving the Winch difficulty aside, unfolded a series of wonderful proposals—proposals he invented as he went along.

Now what those proposals were does not concern the essentials of this story. Suffice it that they were designed in a spirit of infinite benevolence, the sort of benevolence that used to be called post-prandial. Suffice it, too, that the problem of Winch remained unsolved. Nor is it necessary to describe how far that series got to its fulfillment. There were astonishing changes. The small hours found Mr. Maydig and Mr. Fotheringay careering across the chilly market-square under the still moon, in a sort of ecstasy of thaumaturgy, Mr. Maydig all flap and gesture, Mr. Fotheringay short and bristling, and no longer abashed at his greatness. They had reformed every drunkard in the Parliamentary division, changed all the beer and alcohol to water (Mr. Maydig had overruled Mr. Fotheringay on this point), they had, further, greatly improved the railway communication of the place, drained Flinder's swamp, improved the soil of One Tree Hill, and cured the Vicar's wart. And they were going to see what could be done with the injured pier at South Bridge. "The place," gasped Mr. Maydig, "won't be the same place tomorrow. How surprised and thankful everyone will be!" And just at that moment the church clock struck three.

"I say," said Mr. Fotheringay, "that's three o'clock! I must be getting back. I've got to be at business by eight. And besides, Mrs. Wimms——"

"We're only beginning," said Mr. Maydig, full of the sweetness of unlimited power. "We're only beginning. Think of all the good we're doing. When people wake——"

"But——," said Mr. Fotheringay.

Mr. Maydig gripped his arm suddenly. His eyes were bright and wild. "My dear chap," he said, "there's no hurry. Look"—he pointed to the moon at the zenith—"Joshua!"

"Joshua?" said Mr. Fotheringay.

"Joshua," said Mr. Maydig. "Why not? Stop it."

Mr. Fotheringay looked at the moon.

"That's a bit tall," he said after a pause.

"Why not?" said Mr. Maydig. "Of course it doesn't stop. You stop the rotation of the earth, you know. Time stops. It isn't as if we were doing harm."

"H'm!" said Mr. Fotheringay. "Well." He sighed. "I'll try. Here——"

He buttoned up his jacket and addressed himself to the habitable globe, with as good an assumption of confidence as lay in his power. "Jest stop rotating, will you?" said Mr. Fotheringay.

Incontinently he was flying head over heels through the air at the rate of dozens of miles a minute. In spite of the innumerable circles he was describing per second, he thought; for thought is wonderful—sometimes as sluggish as flowing pitch, sometimes as instantaneous as light. He thought in a second, and willed. "Let me come down safe and sound. Whatever else happens, let me down safe and sound."

He willed it only just in time, for his clothes, heated by his rapid flight through the air, were already beginning to singe. He came down with a forcible but by no means injurious bump in what appeared to be a mound of fresh-turned earth. A large mass of metal and masonry, extraordinarily like the clock-tower in the middle of the market-square, hit the earth near him, ricochetted over him, and flew into stonework, bricks, and masonry, like a bursting bomb. A hurtling cow hit one of the larger blocks and smashed like an egg. There was a crash that made all the most violent crashes of his past life seem like the sound of falling dust, and this was followed by a descending series of lesser crashes. A vast wind roared throughout earth and heaven, so that he could scarcely lift his head to look. For a while he was too breathless and astonished even to see where he was or what had happened. And his first movement was to feel his head and reassure himself that his streaming hair was still his own.

"Lord!" gasped Mr. Fotheringay, scarce able to speak for the gale, "I've had a squeak! What's gone wrong? Storms and thunder. And only a minute ago a fine night. It's Maydig set me on to this sort of thing. *What* a wind! If I go on fooling in this way I'm bound to have a thundering accident!...

"Where's Maydig?

"What a confounded mess everything's in!"

He looked about him so far as his flapping jacket would permit. The appearance of things was really extremely strange. "The sky's all right anyhow," said Mr. Fotheringay. "And that's about all that is all right. And even there it looks like a terrific gale coming up. But there's the moon overhead. Just as it was just now. Bright as midday. But as for the rest—— Where's the village? Where's—where's anything? And what on earth set this wind a-blowing? *I* didn't order no wind."

Mr. Fotheringay struggled to get to his feet in vain, and after one failure, remained on all fours, holding on. He surveyed the moonlit world to leeward, with the tails of his jacket streaming over his head. "There's something seriously wrong," said Mr. Fotheringay. "And what it is—goodness knows."

Far and wide nothing was visible in the white glare through the haze of dust that drove before a screaming gale but tumbled masses of earth and heaps of inchoate ruins, no trees, no houses, no familiar shapes, only a wilderness of disorder vanishing at last into the darkness beneath the whirling columns and streamers, the lightnings and thunderings of a swiftly rising storm. Near him in the livid glare was something that might once have been an elm-tree, a smashed mass of splinters, shivered from boughs to base, and further a twisted mass of iron girders—only too evidently the viaduct—rose out of the piled confusion.

You see, when Mr. Fotheringay had arrested the rotation of the solid globe, he had made no stipulation concerning the trifling movables upon its surface. And the earth spins so fast that the surface at its equator is travelling at rather more than a thousand miles an hour, and in these latitudes at more than half that pace. So that the village, and Mr. Maydig, and Mr. Fotheringay, and everybody and everything had been jerked violently forward at about nine miles per second—that is to say, much more violently than if they had been fired out of a cannon. And every human being, every living creature, every house, and every tree—all the world as we know it—had been so jerked and smashed and utterly destroyed. That was all.

These things Mr. Fotheringay did not, of course, fully appreciate. But he perceived that his miracle had miscarried, and with that a great disgust of miracles came upon him. He was in darkness now, for the clouds had swept together and blotted out his momentary glimpse of the moon, and the air was full of fitful struggling tortured wraiths of hail. A great roaring of wind and waters filled earth and sky, and, peering under his hand through the dust and sleet to windward, he saw by the play of the lightnings a vast wall of water pouring towards him.

"Maydig!" screamed Mr. Fotheringay's feeble voice amid the elemental uproar. "Here!—Maydig!"

"Stop!" cried Mr. Fotheringay to the advancing water. "Oh, for goodness' sake, stop!"

"Just a moment," said Mr. Fotheringay to the lightnings and thunder. "Stop jest a moment while I collect my thoughts... And now what shall I do?" he said. "What *shall* I do? Lord! I wish Maydig was about."

"I know," said Mr. Fotheringay. "And for goodness' sake let's have it right *this* time."

He remained on all fours, leaning against the wind, very intent to have everything right.

"Ah!" he said. "Let nothing what I'm going to order happen until I say 'Off!' ... Lord! I wish I'd thought of that before!"

He lifted his little voice against the whirlwind, shouting louder and louder in the vain desire to hear himself speak. "Now then!—here goes! Mind about that what I said just now. In the first place, when all I've got to say is done, let me lose my miraculous power, let my will become just like anybody else's will, and all these dangerous miracles be stopped. I don't like them. I'd rather I didn't work 'em. Ever so much. That's the first thing. And the second is—let me be back just before the miracles begin; let everything be just as it was before that blessed lamp turned up. It's a big job, but it's the last. Have you got it? No more miracles, everything as it was—me back in the Long Dragon just before I drank my half-pint. That's it! Yes."

He dug his fingers into the mould, closed his eyes, and said "Off!"

Everything became perfectly still. He perceived that he was standing erect.

"So *you* say," said a voice.

He opened his eyes. He was in the bar of the Long Dragon, arguing about miracles with Toddy Beamish. He had a vague sense of some great thing forgotten that instantaneously passed. You see, except for the loss of his miraculous powers, everything was back as it had been; his mind and memory therefore were now just as they had been at the time when this story began. So that he knew absolutely nothing of all that is told here, knows nothing of all that is told here to this day. And among other things, of course, he still did not believe in miracles.

"I tell you that miracles, properly speaking, can't possibly happen," he said, "whatever you like to hold. And I'm prepared to prove it up to the hilt."

"That's what *you* think," said Toddy Beamish, and "Prove it if you can."

"Looky here, Mr. Beamish," said Mr. Fotheringay. "Let us clearly understand what a miracle is. It's something contrariwise to the course of nature done by power of Will...."

Appendix II
"A Vision of Judgment,"
by H.G. Wells (1899)

In the Book of Revelation, Last Things are heralded by the Last Trump, when all mankind is brought before God's throne for a final judgment. The present story imagines that event, but with this difference. God lets everybody go to "try again." One member of the gathered throng observes, "There's Darwin. *He'll* catch it!" He doesn't — but mistaken churchmen, who preached against evolution on theological grounds, evidently do.

The Giver of Power in the film story makes the same judgment — try again — after Mr. Fotheringay's devastating mistake. "Come back here in an age or so and you shall see," he says to his fellow elementals. Mankind will in time progress and do better once its emergent elite acts on the Darwinian cosmic perspective.

The story first appeared in the September 1899 issue of *Butterfly*, a now obscure literary periodical.

A VISION OF JUDGMENT

§ 1

BRU-A-A-A.

I listened, not understanding.

Wa-ra-ra-ra.

"Good Lord!" said I, still only half awake. "What an infernal shindy!"

Ra-ra-ra-ra-ra-ra-ra-ra-ra Ta-ra-rra-ra.

"It's enough," said I, "to wake——" and stopped short. Where was I?

Ta-rra-rara—louder and louder.

"It's either some new invention——"

Toora-toora-toora! Deafening!

"No," said I, speaking loud in order to hear myself. "That's the Last Trump."

Tooo-rraa!

§2

The last note jerked me out of my grave like a hooked minnow.

I saw my monument (rather a mean little affair, and I wished I knew who'd done it), and the old elm tree and the sea view vanished like a puff of steam, and then all about me—a multitude no man could number, nations, tongues, kingdoms, peoples—children of all the ages, in an amphitheatral space as vast as the sky. And over against us, seated on a throne of dazzling white cloud, the Lord God and all the host of his angels. I recognized Azreal by his darkness and Michael by his sword, and the great angel who had blown the trumpet stood with the trumpet still half raised.

§3

"Prompt," said the little man beside me. "Very prompt. Do you see the angel with the book?"

He was ducking and craning his head about to see over and under and between the souls that crowded around us. "Everybody's here," he said. "Everybody. And now we shall know——

"There's Darwin," he said, going off at a tangent. "*He'll* catch it! And there—you see?—that tall, important-looking man trying to catch the eye of the Lord God, that's the Duke. But there's a lot of people one doesn't know.

"Oh! there's Priggles, the publisher. I have always wondered about printers' overs. Priggles was a clever man.... But we shall know now—even about him.

"I shall hear all that. I shall get most of the fun before.... *My* letter's S."

He drew the air in between his teeth.

"Historical characters, too. See? That's Henry the Eighth. There'll be a good bit of evidence. Oh, damn! He's Tudor."

He lowered his voice. "Notice this chap, just in front of us, all covered with hair. Paleolithic, you know. And there again——"

But I did not heed him, because I was looking at the Lord God.

§4

"Is this *all*?" asked the Lord God.

The angel at the book—it was one of countless volumes, like the British Museum Reading-room Catalogue, glanced at us and seemed to count us in the instant.

"That's all," he said, and added: "It was, O God, a very little planet."

The eyes of God surveyed us.

"Let us begin," said the Lord God.

§5

The angel opened the book and read a name. It was a name full of A's, and the echoes of it came back out of the uttermost parts of space. I did not catch it clearly, because the little man beside me said, in a sharp jerk, "*What's* that?" It sounded like "Ahab" to me; but it could not have been the Ahab of Scripture.

Instantly a small black figure was lifted up to a puffy cloud at the very feet of God. It was a stiff little figure, dressed in rich outlandish robes and crowned, and it folded its arms and scowled.

"Well?" said God, looking down at him.

We were privileged to hear the reply, and indeed the acoustic properties of the place were marvellous.

"I plead guilty," said the little figure.

"Tell them what you have done," said the Lord God.

"I was a king," said the little figure, "a great king, and I was lustful and proud and cruel. I made wars, I devastated countries, I built palaces, and the mortar was the blood of men. Hear, O God, the witnesses against me, calling to you for vengeance. Hundreds and thousands of witnesses." He waved his hands towards us. "and worse! I took a prophet—one of your prophets——"

"One of my prophets," said the Lord God.

"And because he would not bow to me, I tortured him for four days and nights, and in the end he died. I did more, O God, I blasphemed. I robbed you of your honours——"

"Robbed me of my honours," said the Lord God.

"I caused myself to be worshipped in your stead. No evil was there but I practised it; no cruelty wherewith I did not stain my soul. And at last you smote me, O God!"

God raised his eyebrows slightly.

"And I was slain in battle. And so I stand before you, meet for your nethermost Hell! Out of your greatness daring no lies, daring no pleas, but telling the truth of my iniquities before all mankind."

He ceased. His face I saw distinctly, and it seemed to me white and terrible and proud and strangely noble. I thought of Milton's Satan.

"Most of that is from the Obelisk," said the Recording Angel, finger on page.

"It is," said the Tyrannous Man, with a faint touch of surprise.

Then suddenly God bent forward and took this man in his hand, and held him up on his palm as if to see him better. He was just a little dark stroke in the middle of God's palm.

"*Did* he do all this?" said the Lord God.

The Recording Angel flattened his book with his hand.

"In a way," said the Recording Angel, carelessly.

Now when I looked again at the little man his face had changed in a very curious manner. He was looking at the Recording Angel with a strange apprehension in his eyes, and one hand fluttered to his mouth. Just the movement of a muscle or so, and all that dignity of defiance was gone.

"Read," said the Lord God.

And the angel read, explaining very carefully and fully all the wickedness of the Wicked Man. It was quite an intellectual treat.—A little "daring" in places, I thought, but of course Heaven has its privileges....

§6

Everybody was laughing. Even the prophet of the Lord whom the Wicked Man had tortured had a smile on his face. The Wicked Man was really such a preposterous little fellow.

"And then," read the Recording Angel, with a smile that set us all agog, "one day, when he was a little irascible from over-eating, he——"'

"Oh, not *that*," cried the Wicked Man, "nobody knew of *that*.

"It didn't happen," screamed the Wicked Man. "I was bad—I was really bad. Frequently bad, but there was nothing so silly—so absolutely silly——"

The angel went on reading.

"O God!" cried the Wicked Man. "Don't let them know that! I'll repent! I'll apologise...."

The Wicked Man on God's hand began to dance and weep. Suddenly shame overcame him. He made a wild rush to jump off the ball of God's little finger, but God stopped him by a dexterous turn of the wrist. Then he made a rush for the gap between hand and thumb, but the thumb closed. And all the while the angel went on reading—reading. The Wicked Man rushed to and fro across God's palm, and then suddenly turned about and fled up the sleeve of God.

I expected God would turn him out, but the mercy of God is infinite. The Recording Angel paused.

"Eh?" said the Recording Angel.

"Next," said God, and before the Recording Angel could call upon the name a hairy creature in filthy rags stood upon God's palm.

§7

"Has God got Hell up his sleeve then?" said the little man beside me.

"Is there a Hell?" I asked.

"If you notice," he said—he peered between the feet of the great angels—"there's no particular indication of the Celestial City."

"'Ssh!" said a little woman near us, scowling. "Hear this blessed Saint!"

§8

"He was Lord of the Earth, but I was the prophet of the god of Heaven," cried the Saint, "and all the people marvelled at the sign. For I, O God, knew of the glories of thy Paradise. No pain, no hardship, gashing with knives, splinters thrust under my nails, strips of flesh flayed off, all for the glory and honour of God."

God smiled.

"And at last I went, I in my rags and sores, smelling of my holy discomforts——"

Gabriel laughed abruptly.

"And lay outside his gates, as a sign, as a wonder——"

"As a perfect nuisance," said the Recording Angel, and began to read, heedless of the fact that the Saint was still speaking of the gloriously unpleasant things he had done that Paradise might be his.

And behold, in that book the record of the Saint also was a revelation, a marvel.

It seemed not ten seconds before the Saint also was rushing to and fro over the great palm of God. Not ten seconds! And at last he also shrieked beneath that pitiless and cynical exposition, and fled also, even as the Wicked Man had fled, into the shadow of the sleeve. And it was permitted us to see into the shadow of the sleeve. And the two sat side by side, stark of all delusions, in the shadow of the robe of God's charity, like brothers.

And thither also I fled in my turn.

§9

"And now," said God, as he shook us out of his sleeve upon the planet he had given us to live upon, the planet that whirled about green Sirius for a sun, "now that you understand me and each other a little better, ... try again."

Then he and his great angels turned themselves about and suddenly had vanished.

The Throne had vanished.

All about me was a beautiful land, more beautiful than any I had ever seen before—waste, austere, and wonderful; and all about me were the enlightened souls of men in new clean bodies....

Appendix III
"Under the Knife,"
by H.G. Wells (1896)

In this powerful story, unlike anything else in English letters, Wells makes vivid his abstract sense of cosmic vision with startling imagery. It conveys his deepest conviction that, if mankind is to be saved from itself, from the animal-like pain/pleasure principle that drives it, true statesmen must think in the fourth dimension of all space and time. Such are the men of knowledge and power who guide human destiny in *Things to Come*.

A patient under ether for surgery experiences astral projection. Stripped of the "garments of flesh," he rises amidst the distant stars and galaxies to become a naked intelligence, unemotional, detached, observant. The last line, "There will be no more pain," the physician's when the patient recovers, echoes the Book of Revelation. For selfless saints, after the Last Judgment, there will indeed be no more pain nor any further suffering of the limiting human condition.

The story first appeared in the January 1896 issue of the *New Review*.

UNDER THE KNIFE

"WHAT if I die under it?" The thought recurred again and again as I walked home from Haddon's. It was a purely personal question. I was spared the deep anxieties of a married man, and I knew there were few of my intimate friends but would find my death troublesome chiefly on account of their duty of regret. I was surprised indeed and perhaps a little humiliated, as I turned the matter over, to think how few could possibly exceed the conventional requirement. Things came before me stripped of glamour, in a clear dry light, during that walk from Haddon's house over Primrose Hill. There were the friends of my youth; I perceived now that our affection was a tradition which we foregathered rather laboriously to maintain. There were the rivals and helpers of my later career: I suppose I had been cold-blooded or undemonstrative—one perhaps implies the other. It may be that even the capacity for friendship is a question of physique. There had been a time in my own life when I had grieved bitterly enough at the loss of a friend; but as I walked home that afternoon the emotional side of my imagination was dormant. I could not pity myself, nor feel sorry for my friends, nor conceive of them as grieving for me.

I was interested in this deadness of my emotional nature—no doubt a concomitant of my stagnating physiology; and my thoughts wandered off along the line it suggested. Once before, in my hot youth, I had suffered a sudden loss of blood and had been within an ace of death. I remembered now that my affections as well as my passions had drained out of me, leaving scarcely anything but a tranquil resignation, a dreg of self-pity. It had been weeks before the old ambitions, and tendernesses, and all the complex moral interplay of a man, had reasserted themselves. Now again I was bloodless; I had been feeling down for a week or more. I was not even hungry. It occurred to me that the real meaning of this numbness might be a gradual slipping away from the pleasure-pain guidance of the animal man. It has been proven, I take it, as thoroughly as anything can be proven in the world, that the higher emotions, the moral feelings, even the subtle tendernesses of love, are evolved from the elemental desires and fears of the simple animal: they are the harness in which man's mental freedom goes. And it may be that, as death overshadows us, as our possibility of acting diminishes, this complex growth of balanced impulse, propensity, and aversion whose interplay inspires our acts, goes with it. Leaving what?

I was suddenly brought back to reality by an imminent collision with a butcher-boy's tray. I found that I was crossing the bridge over Regent's Park Canal which runs parallel with that in the Zoölogical Gardens. The boy in blue had been looking over his shoulder at a black barge advancing slowly, towed by a gaunt white horse. In the Gardens a nurse was leading three happy little children over the bridge. The trees were bright green; the spring hopefulness was still unstrained by the dusts of summer; the sky in the water was bright and clear, but broken by long waves, by quivering bands of black, as the barge drove through. The breeze was stirring; but it did not stir me as the spring breeze used to do.

Was this dulness of feeling in itself an anticipation? It was curious that I could reason and follow out a network of suggestion as clearly as ever: so, at least, it seemed to me. It was calmness rather than dulness that was coming upon me. Was there any ground for the belief in the presentiment of death? Did a man near to death begin instinctively to withdraw himself from the meshes of matter and sense, even before the cold hand was laid upon his? I felt strangely isolated—isolated without regret—from the life and existence about me. The children playing in the sun and gathering strength and experience for the business of life, the park-keeper gossiping with a nursemaid, the nursing mother, the young couple intent upon each other as they passed me, the trees by the wayside spreading new pleading leaves to the sunlight, the stir in their branches—I had been part of it all, but I had nearly done with it now.

Some way down the Broad Walk I perceived that I was tired, and that my feet were heavy. It was hot that afternoon, and I turned aside and sat down on one of the green chairs that line the way. In a minute I had dozed into a dream, and the tide of my thoughts washed up a vision of the resurrection. I was still sitting in the chair, but I thought myself actually dead, withered, tattered, dried, one eye (I saw) pecked out by birds. "Awake!" cried a voice; and incontinently the dust of the path and the mould under the grass became insurgent. I had never before thought of Regent's Park as a cemetery, but now through the trees, stretching as far as eye could see, I beheld a flat plain of writhing graves and heeling tombstones. There seemed to be some trouble: the rising dead appeared to stifle as they struggled upward, they bled in their struggles, the red flesh was tattered away from the white bones. "Awake!" cried a voice; but I determined I would not rise to such horrors. "Awake!" They would not let me alone. "Wike up!" said an angry voice. A cockney angel! The man who sells the tickets was shaking me, demanding my penny.

I paid my penny, pocketed my ticket, yawned, stretched my legs, and, feeling now rather less torpid, got up and walked on towards Langham Place. I speedily lost myself again in a shifting maze of thoughts about death. Going across Marylebone Road into that crescent at the end of Langham Place, I had the narrowest escape from the shaft of a cab, and went on my way with a palpitating heart and a bruised shoulder. It struck me that it would have been curious if my meditations on my death on the morrow had led to my death that day.

But I will not weary you with more of my experiences that day and the next. I knew more and more certainly that I should die under the operation; at times I think I was inclined to pose to myself. At home I found everything prepared; my room cleared of needless objects and hung with white sheets; a nurse installed and already at loggerheads with my housekeeper. They wanted me to go to bed early, and after a little resistance I obeyed.

In the morning I was very indolent, and though I read my newspapers and the letters that came by the first post, I did not find them very interesting. There was a friendly note from Addison, my old school friend, calling my attention to two discrepancies and a printer's error in my new book, with one from Langridge venting some vexation over Minton. The rest were business communications. I had a cup of tea but nothing to eat. The glow of pain at my side seemed more massive. I knew it was pain, and yet, if you can understand, I did not find it very painful. I had been awake and hot and thirsty in the night, but in the morning bed felt comfortable. In the night-time I had lain thinking of things that were past; in the morning I dozed over the question of immortality. Haddon came, punctual to the minute, with a neat black bag; and Mowbray soon followed. Their arrival stirred me up a little. I began to take a more personal interest in the proceedings. Haddon moved the little octagonal table close to the bedside, and, with his broad black back to me, began taking things out of his bag. I heard the light click of steel upon steel. My imagination, I found, was not altogether stagnant. "Will you hurt me much?" I said in an off-hand tone.

"Not a bit," Haddon answered over his shoulder. "We shall chloroform you. Your heart's as sound as a bell." And as he spoke I had a whiff of the pungent sweetness of the anæsthetic.

They stretched me out, with a convenient exposure of my side, and, almost before I realised what was happening, the chloroform was being administered. It stings the nostrils, and there is a suffocating sensation, at first. I knew I should die—that this was the end of consciousness for me. And suddenly I felt that I was not prepared for death: I had a vague sense of a duty overlooked—I knew not what. What was it I had not done? I could think of nothing more to do, nothing desirable left in life; and yet I had the strangest disinclination for death. And the physical sensation was painfully oppressive. Of course the doctors did not know they were going to kill me. Possibly I struggled. Then I fell motionless, and a great silence, a monstrous silence, and an impenetrable blackness came upon me.

There must have been an interval of absolute unconsciousness, seconds or minutes. Then, with a chilly, unemotional clearness, I perceived that I was not yet dead. I was still in my body; but all the multitudinous sensations that come sweeping from it to make up the background of consciousness had gone, leaving me free of it all. No, not free of it all; for as yet something still held me to the poor stark flesh upon the bed—held me, yet not so closely that I did not feel myself external to it, independent of it, straining away from it. I do not think I saw, I do not think I heard; but I perceived all that was going on, and it was as if I both heard and saw. Haddon was bending over me, Mowbray behind me; the scalpel—it was a large scalpel—was cutting my flesh at the side under the flying ribs. It was interesting to see myself cut like cheese, without a pang, without even a qualm. The interest was much of a quality with that one might feel in a game of chess between strangers. Haddon's face was firm and his hand steady; but I was surprised to perceive (*how* I know not) that he was feeling the gravest doubt as to his own wisdom in the conduct of the operation.

Mowbray's thoughts, too, I could see. He was thinking that Haddon's manner showed too much of the specialist. New suggestions came up like bubbles through a stream of frothing meditation, and burst one after another in the little bright spot of his consciousness. He could not help noticing and admiring Haddon's swift dexterity, in spite of his envious quality and his disposition to detract. I saw my liver exposed. I was puzzled at my own condition. I did not feel that I was dead, but I was different in some way from my living self. The grey depression that had weighed on me for a year or more and coloured all my thoughts, was gone. I perceived and thought without any emotional tint at all. I wondered if everyone perceived things in this way under chloroform, and forgot it again when he came out of it. It would be inconvenient to look into some heads, and not forget.

Although I did not think that I was dead, I still perceived quite clearly that I was soon to die. This brought me back to the consideration of Haddon's proceedings. I looked into his mind, and saw that he was afraid of cutting a branch of the portal vein. My attention was distracted from details by the curious changes going on in his mind. His consciousness was like the quivering little spot of light which is thrown by the mirror of a galvanometer. His thoughts ran under it like a stream, some through the focus bright and distinct, some shadowy in the half-light of the edge. Just now the little glow was steady; but the least movement on Mowbray's part, the slightest sound from outside, even a faint difference in the slow movement of the living flesh he was cutting, set the light-spot shivering and spinning. A new sense-impression came rushing up through the flow of thoughts, and lo! the light-spot jerked away towards it, swifter than a frightened fish. It was wonderful to think that upon that unstable, fitful thing depended all the complex motions of the man; that for the next five minutes, therefore, my life hung upon its movements. And he was growing more and more nervous in his work. It was as if a little picture of a cut vein grew brighter, and struggled to oust from his brain another picture of a cut falling short of the mark. He was afraid: his dread of cutting too little was battling with his dread of cutting too far.

Then, suddenly, like an escape of water from under a lock-gate, a great uprush of horrible realisation set all his thoughts swirling, and simultaneously I perceived that the vein was cut. He started back with a hoarse exclamation, and I saw the brown-purple blood gather in a swift bead, and run trickling. He was horrified. He pitched the red stained scalpel on to the octagonal table; and instantly both doctors flung themselves upon me, making hasty and ill-conceived efforts to remedy the disaster. "Ice!" said Mowbray, gasping. But I knew that I was killed, though my body still clung to me.

I will not describe their belated endeavours to save me, though I perceived every detail. My perceptions were sharper and swifter than they had ever been in life; my thoughts rushed through my mind with incredible swiftness, but with perfect definition. I can only compare their crowded clarity to the effects of a reasonable dose of opium. In a moment it would all be over, and I should be free. I knew I was immortal, but what would happen I did not know. Should I drift off presently, like a puff of smoke from a gun, in some kind of half-material body, an attenuated version of my material self? Should I find myself suddenly among the innumerable hosts of the dead, and know the world about me for the phantasmagoria it had always seemed? Should I drift to some spiritualistic *séance*, and there make foolish, incomprehensible attempts to affect a purblind medium? It was a state of unemotional curiosity, of colourless expectation. And then I realised a growing stress upon me, a feeling as though some huge human magnet was drawing me upward out of my body. The stress grew and grew. I seemed an atom for which monstrous forces were fighting. For one brief, terrible moment sensation came back to me. That feeling of falling headlong which comes in nightmares, that feeling a thousand times intensified, that and a black horror swept across my thoughts in a torrent. Then the two doctors, the naked body with its cut side, the little room, swept away from under me and vanished as a speck of foam vanishes down an eddy.

I was in mid-air. Far below was the West End of London, receding rapidly,—for I seemed to be flying swiftly upward,—and, as it receded, passing westward, like a panorama. I could see, through the faint haze of smoke, the innumerable roofs chimney-set, the narrow roadways stippled with people and conveyances, the little specks of squares, and the church steeples like thorns sticking out of the fabric. But it spun away as the earth rotated on its axis, and in a few seconds (as it seemed) I was over the scattered clumps of town about Ealing, the little Thames a thread of blue to the south, and the Chiltern Hills and the North Downs coming up like the rim of a basin, far away and faint with haze. Up I rushed. And at first I had not the faintest conception what this headlong rush upward could mean.

Every moment the circle of scenery beneath me grew wider and wider, and the details of town and field, of hill and valley, got more and more hazy and pale and indistinct, a luminous grey was mingled more and more with the blue of the hills and the green of the open meadows; and a little patch of cloud, low and far to the west, shone ever more dazzlingly white. Above, as the veil of atmosphere between myself and outer space grew thinner, the sky, which had been a fair springtime blue at first, grew deeper and richer in colour, passing steadily through the intervening shades until presently it was as dark as the blue sky of midnight, and presently as black as the blackness of a frosty starlight, and at last as black as no blackness I had ever beheld. And first one star and then many, and at last an innumerable host broke out upon the sky: more stars than anyone has ever seen from the face of the earth. For the blueness of the sky is the light of the sun and stars sifted and spread abroad blindingly: there is diffused light even in the darkest skies of winter, and we do not see the stars by day only because of the dazzling irradiation of the sun. But now I saw things—I know not how; assuredly with no mortal eyes—and that defect of bedazzlement blinded me no longer. The sun was incredibly strange and wonderful. The body of it was a disc of blinding white light: not yellowish as it seems to those who live upon the earth, but livid white, all streaked with scarlet streaks and rimmed about with a fringe of writhing tongues of red fire. And, shooting halfway across the heavens from either side of it, and brighter than the Milky Way, were two pinions of silver-white, making it look more like those winged globes I have seen in Egyptian sculpture than anything else I can remember upon earth. These I knew for the solar corona, though I had never seen anything of it but a picture during the days of my earthly life.

When my attention came back to the earth again, I saw that it had fallen very far away from me. Field and town were long since indistinguishable, and all the varied hues of the country were emerging into a uniform bright grey, broken only by the brilliant white of the clouds that lay scattered in flocculent masses over Ireland and the west of England. For now I could see the outlines of the north of France and Ireland, and all this island of Britain save where Scotland passed over the horizon to the north, or where the coast was blurred or obliterated by cloud. The sea was a dull grey, and darker than the land; and the whole panorama was rotating slowly towards the east.

All this had happened so swiftly that, until I was some thousand miles or so from the earth, I had no thought for myself. But now I perceived I had neither hands nor feet, neither parts nor organs, and that I felt neither alarm nor pain. All about me I perceived that the vacancy (for I had already left the air behind) was cold beyond the imagination of man; but it troubled me not. The sun's rays shot through the void, powerless to light or head until they should strike on matter in their course. I saw things with a serene self-forgetfulness, even as if I were God. And down below there, rushing away from me,—countless miles in a second,—where a little dark spot on the grey marked the position of London, two doctors were struggling to restore life to the poor hacked and outworn shell I had abandoned. I felt then such release, such serenity as I can compare to no mortal delight I have ever known.

It was only after I had perceived all these things that the meaning of that headlong rush of the earth grew into comprehension. Yet it was so simple, so obvious, that I was amazed at my never anticipating the thing that was happening to me. I had suddenly been cut adrift from matter: all that was material of me was there upon earth, whirling away through space, held to the earth by gravitation, partaking of the earth's inertia, moving in its wreath of epicycles round the sun, and with the sun and the planets on their vast march through space. But the immaterial has no inertia, feels nothing of the pull of matter for matter: where it parts from its garments of flesh, there it remains (so far as space concerns it any longer) immovable in space. *I* was not leaving the earth: the earth was leaving *me*, and not only the earth, but the whole solar system was streaming past. And about me in space, invisible to me, scattered in the wake of the earth upon its journey, there must be an innumerable multitude of souls, stripped like myself of the material, stripped like myself of the passions of the individual and the generous emotions of the gregarious brute, naked intelligences, things of newborn wonder and thought, marvelling at the strange release that had suddenly come on them!

As I receded faster and faster from the strange white sun in the black heavens, and from the broad and shining earth upon which my being had begun, I seemed to grow, in some incredible manner, vast: vast as regards this world I had left, vast as regards the moments and periods of a human life. Very soon I saw the full circle of the earth, slightly gibbous, like the moon when she nears her full, but very large; and the silvery shape of America was now in the noonday blaze wherein (as it seemed) little England had been basking but minutes ago. At first the earth was large and shone in the heavens, filling a great part of them; but every moment she grew smaller and more distant. As she shrunk, the broad moon in its third quarter crept into view over the rim of her disc. I looked for the constellations. Only that part of Aries directly behind the sun, and the Lion, which the earth covered, were hidden. I recognised the tortuous, tattered band of the Milky Way, with Vega very bright between sun and earth; and Sirius and Orion shone splendid against the unfathomable blackness in the opposite quarter of the heavens. The Pole Star was overhead, and the Great Bear hung over the circle of the earth. And away beneath and beyond the shining corona of the sun were strange groupings of stars I had never seen in my life—notably, a dagger-shaped group that I knew for the Southern Cross. All these were no larger than when they had shone on earth; but the little stars that one scarcely sees shone now against the setting of black vacancy as brightly as the first-magnitudes had done, while the larger worlds were points of indescribable glory and colour. Aldebaran was a spot of blood-red fire, and Sirius condensed to one point the light of a world of sapphires. And they shone steadily: they did not scintillate, they were calmly glorious. My impressions had an adamantine hardness and brightness: there was no blurring softness, no atmosphere, nothing but infinite darkness set with the myriads of these acute and brilliant points and specks of light. Presently, when I looked again, the little earth seemed no bigger than the sun, and it dwindled and turned as I looked until, in a second's space (as it seemed to me), it was halved; and so it went on swiftly dwindling. Far away in the opposite direction, a little pinkish pin's head of light, shining steadily, was the planet Mars. I swam motionless in vacancy, and, without a trace of terror or astonishment, watched the speck of cosmic dust we call the world fall away from me.

Presently it dawned upon me that my sense of duration had changed: that my mind was moving not faster but infinitely slower, that between each separate impression there was a period of many days. The moon spun once round the earth as I noted this; and I perceived clearly the motion of Mars in his orbit. Moreover, it appeared as if the time between thought and thought grew steadily greater, until at last, a thousand years was but a moment in my perception.

At first the constellations had shone motionless against the black background of infinite space; but presently it seemed as though the group of stars about Hercules and the Scorpion was contracting, while Orion and Aldebaran and their neighbours were scattering apart. Flashing suddenly out of the darkness there came a flying multitude of particles of rock, glittering like dust specks in a sunbeam, and encompassed in a faintly luminous haze. They swirled all about me, and vanished again in a twinkling far behind. And then I saw that a bright spot of light, that shone a little to one side of my path, was growing very rapidly larger, and perceived that it was the planet Saturn rushing towards me. Larger and larger it grew, swallowing up the heavens behind it, and hiding every moment a fresh multitude of stars. I perceived its flattened, whirling body, its disc-like belt, and seven of its little satellites. It grew and grew, till it towered enormous; and then I plunged amid a streaming multitude of clashing stones and dancing dust-particles and gas-eddies, and saw for a moment the mighty triple belt like three concentric arches of moonlight above me, its shadow black on the boiling tumult below. These things happened in one-tenth of the time it takes to tell of them. The planet went by like a flash of lightning; for a few seconds it blotted out the sun, and there and then became a mere black, dwindling, winged patch against the light. The earth, the mother mote of my being, I could no longer see.

So with a stately swiftness, in the profoundest silence, the solar system fell from me, as it had been a garment, until the sun was a mere star amid the multitude of stars, with its eddy of planet-specks, lost in the confused glittering of the remoter light. I was no longer a denizen of the solar system: I had come to the Outer Universe. I seemed to grasp and comprehend the whole world of matter. Ever more swiftly the stars closed in about the spot where Antares and Vega had vanished in a luminous haze, until that part of the sky had the semblance of a whirling mass of nebulæ, and ever before me yawned vaster gaps of vacant blackness and the stars shone fewer and fewer. It seemed as if I moved towards a point between Orion's belt and sword: and the void about that region opened vaster and vaster every second, an incredible gulf of nothingness, into which I was falling. Faster and ever faster the universe rushed by, a hurry of whirling motes at last, speeding silently into the void. Stars glowing brighter and brighter, with their circling planets catching the light in a ghostly fashion as I neared them, shone out and vanished again into inexistence; faint comets, clusters of meteorites, winking specks of matter, eddying light-points, whizzed past, some perhaps a hundred millions of miles or so from me at most, few nearer, travelling with unimaginable rapidity, shooting constellations, momentary darts of fire, through that black, enormous night. More than anything else it was like a dusty draught, sunbeam-lit. Broader, and wider, and deeper grew the starless space, the vacant Beyond, into which I was being drawn. At last a quarter of the heavens was black and blank, and the whole headlong rush of stellar universe closed in behind me like a veil of light that is gathered together. It drove away from me like a monstrous jack-o'-lantern driven by the wind. I had come out into the wilderness of space. Ever the vacant blackness grew broader, until the hosts of the stars seemed only like a swarm of fiery specks hurrying away from me, inconceivably remote, and the darkness, the nothingness and emptiness, was about me on every side. Soon the little universe of matter, the cage of points in which I had begun to be, was dwindling, now to a whirling disc of luminous glittering, and now to one minute disc of hazy light. In a little while it would shrink to a point, and at last would vanish altogether.

Suddenly feeling came back to me—feeling in the shape of overwhelming terror: such a dread of those dark vastitudes as no words can describe, a passionate resurgence of sympathy and social desire. Were there other souls, invisible to me as I to them, about me in the blackness? or was I indeed, even as I felt, alone? Had I passed out of being into something that was neither being nor not-being? The covering of the body, the covering of matter, had been torn from me, and the hallucinations of companionship and security. Everything was black and silent. I had ceased to be. I was nothing. There was nothing, save only that infinitesimal dot of light that dwindled in the gulf. I strained myself to hear and see, and for a while there was naught but infinite silence, intolerable darkness, horror, and despair.

Then I saw that about the spot of light into which the whole world of matter had shrunk there was a faint glow. And in a band on either side of that the darkness was not absolute. I watched it for ages, as it seemed to me, and through the long waiting the haze grew imperceptibly more distinct. And then about the band appeared an irregular cloud of the faintest, palest brown. I felt a passionate impatience; but the things grew brighter so slowly that they scarcely seemed to change. What was unfolding itself? What was this strange reddish dawn in the interminable night of space?

The cloud's shape was grotesque. It seemed to be looped along its lower side into four projecting masses, and, above, it ended in a straight line. What phantom was it? I felt assured I had seen that figure before; but I could not think what, nor where, nor when it was. Then the realisation rushed upon me. *It was a clenched Hand.* I was alone in space, along with this huge, shadowy Hand, upon which the whole Universe of Matter lay like an unconsidered speck of dust. It seemed as though I watched it through vast periods of time. On the forefinger glittered a ring; and the universe from which I had come was but a spot of light upon the ring's curvature. And the thing that the hand gripped had the likeness of a black rod. Through a long eternity I watched this Hand, with the ring and the rod, marvelling and fearing and waiting helplessly on what might follow. It seemed as though nothing could follow: that I should watch for ever, seeing only the Hand and the thing it held, and understanding nothing of its import. Was the whole universe but a refracting speck upon some greater Being? Were our worlds but the atoms of another universe, and those again of another, and so on through an endless progression? And what was I? Was I indeed immaterial? A vague persuasion of a body gathering about me came into my suspense. The abysmal darkness about the Hand filled with impalpable suggestions, with uncertain, fluctuating shapes.

Came a sound, like the sound of a tolling bell; faint, as if infinitely far, muffled as though heard through thick swathings of darkness: a deep, vibrating resonance, with vast gulfs of silence between each stroke. And the Hand appeared to tighten on the rod. And I saw far above the Hand, towards the apex of the darkness, a circle of dim phosphorescence, a ghostly sphere whence these sounds came throbbing; and at the last stroke the Hand vanished, for the hour had come, and I heard a noise of many waters. But the black rod remained as a great band across the sky. And then a voice, which seemed to run to the uttermost parts of space, spoke, saying, "There will be no more pain."

At that an almost intolerable gladness and radiance rushed upon me, and I saw the circle shining white and bright, and the rod black and shining, and many things else distinct and clear. And the circle was the face of the clock, and the rod the rail of my bed. Haddon was standing at the foot, against the rail, with a small pair of scissors on his fingers; and the hands of my clock on the mantel over his shoulder were clasped together over the hour of twelve. Mowbray was washing something in a basin at the octagonal table, and at my side I felt a subdued feeling that could scarce be spoken of as pain.

The operation had not killed me. And I perceived, suddenly, that the dull melancholy of half a year was lifted from my mind.

Appendix IV
["If I Were Dictator of the World"], by H.G. Wells (1931)

The following is excerpted from a September 1931 BBC radio broadcast, "What I Would Do with the World." Using the version published as Chapter XII in *After Democracy* (1932), I have edited out only some tedious throat-clearing preliminaries before Wells gets down to posing his big question, which he answers in a most revealing way, as reflected in my not inaccurate retitling of the present excerpt.

The question relates to the cosmic issue of world peace (see textual note 42). What if Wells himself had Mr. Fotheringay's power to take charge of the world, but with the same limits the Giver of Power gives *him*? He would do it very differently, more like Oswald Cabal the world dictator in *Things to Come*.

But of course Wells is no Oswald Cabal, heir to John Cabal the great Air Dictator. He can only influence others to accomplish his world state, the point of his radio broadcast. He addresses like-minded people, the common man pointedly excluded, to get together, like those "little grains of gold" identified in textual note 46, and thus form the emergent elite.

Wells touches upon a significant topical issue of the day, Stalin's Five Year Plan announced in 1927, after succeeding to Lenin's founding dictatorship. Wells glorifies this Plan in the previous chapter to the same book, "Russia and the World." Now, in the Soviet Union, "there will be one owner, one single capitalist — the State — and everyone else will be an employee or a pensioner or a prisoner of that supreme power" (1932:182). The Soviet Union models the coming capitalist world state of Wells's utopian dream: the story of *Things to Come*, a companion film to *Miracles* for good reason.

WHAT I WOULD DO WITH THE WORLD

AND now to the question. It is this:—First a hypothesis: "You are to suppose you are Dictator of the world for the next twenty years. All the world is exactly as it is, except that you are Dictator. You have no miraculous power and you have no direct power over the hearts and imaginations of men. You cannot make people love one another or believe in Mahomet for example, but, *never mind how*, people will obey you just as all law-abiding people obey constituted authority. They may not like to obey, but they will do so for the term of your Dictatorship. You have unlimited legislative and administrative power." Then comes the question:—

"*What would you do with the world?* Would you abolish war? And if so how would you set about it, and how would you arrange to leave things at the end of your Dictatorship to prevent its recurrence? Would you make any great changes in the economic methods of mankind? Would you make a Twenty Years' Plan? Would you do anything about money? Would you make any great changes in the biological life of mankind—that is to say, in regard to health, population, and race? Would you do anything to the existing educational methods of mankind?"

That is my patent question, or, if you prefer it, that is my patent group of questions. Essentially it is intended to be a *head-clearing* question amidst our present confusions and anxieties. I submit to you that, unless you have an answer to this question and its various branches, you are not really qualified to vote in an election, much less to take any more important part in public affairs. For what is the good of pushing a cart when you do not know where you are pushing it?

Well, I have tried my question on myself, and I will give you my answer. It may not be a very good answer in your opinion, and in that case I ask you to make another. But I submit you have no right to turn down my answer unless you have a better one. So herewith at the microphone I assume the World Dictatorship—I am only the first of a series of World Dictators who will announce their policies through the B.B.C.—and do my best to tell you what I would do with the world if I had unlimited legislative and administrative power—but no power (we must bear that in mind) over the hearts and faith of men.

Would I abolish war? Yes. Many people think that war cannot be abolished, but I am not of that opinion. Some fierce and strenuous souls would not abolish it if they could. They regard war as the supreme sport in life. That is a question of taste, and my taste is not for tragedy and triumph. I would abolish war. But simply to abolish war is nothing very much. Mr. Kellogg abolished war a year or so ago—without any marked results. War still hangs over us, as threateningly as ever. In Mukden, in South Manchuria, the other day it seemed quite pre-Kellogg times. And so I have to go on to tell *how* I would abolish war, what sort of abolition I contemplate. To my mind, war will be effectively abolished only when the sovereign states of the world relinquish so much of the national sovereignty as to place the control of their relations one to another in the hands of a federal world authority, a Peace Council. So long as they are free to make war they will do so. This Peace Council would not be anything so elaborate in its constitution as the League of Nations, but it would be given much more power. I do not know whether I should make trouble at first to assemble representatives of more than, say, the eight or nine greater governments in that Council. The others would gravitate in later. This Council would be plainly a super-government, which would pool the Foreign Offices and diplomatic services of its constituents. It would also be a permanent Disarmament Committee; it would pool the military, naval, and air establishments of the federated nations into one international force, and proceed to reduce that force to the dimensions of a world police.

Do not tell me that no power, no independent country would stand that. Remember that for the purposes of this talk I am World Dictator with a tenure of twenty years. I am not talking of what people or nations or governments will or will not stand. I am talking of what I would dictate. I am telling you what I consider desirable and what I would do if I could over-ride governments as some day, I hope, the common-sense of mankind *will* override governments. I should pool, not only the foreign offices and diplomatic services of the world, but also the arsenals, dockyards, war offices, navies, and air forces of the world, and cut them down. It would be an immense task, but not so very much greater than the scrapping and disbanding that went on after the War. There would be a methodical, progressive amalgamation, scrapping, disbandment, paying off, and pensioning off of these vast establishments. At the end of my twenty years of power the world would be free, of course, to restore them and put these mighty organizations together again—if it could.

But my Peace Council and that real and genuine permanent Disarmament Commission could not stand by themselves. It is nonsense—such nonsense that only eminent politicians have the impudence to talk it—to contemplate disarmament and the abolition of war while leaving nations engaged, as they are engaged now, in the most strenuous and subtle economic and financial struggles. If you agree with the policy of dictatorship so far, you will agree to my second parallel project, which will be to set up, side by side with my World Peace and Disarmament Council, a second body for the reorganization of our financial and economic life on a world scale. It is really nothing more than what our statesmen and men of affairs are feeling their way towards to-day—too timidly and slowly, I fear—with their Debt conferences, the Bank of International Settlements, and so forth. As World Dictators, you or I can travel faster. They have to go slowly because they have to follow the spread of new ideas. We Dictators can lead ideas. My World Economic Council would make a Twenty Years' Plan for the reorganization of the world's production and distribution. It would not smash down all the tariff walls at once—that might lead to frightful convulsions—but it would set about reducing them methodically, organizing the transport of the world by sea and land and air as one system, assigning types of cultivation and manufacture to the most favourable regions, possibly shifting workers to new regions of employment, irrigating deserts, and restoring forests. It would obviously be a Council with a big personnel; I should get every disinterested industrial and agricultural organizer I could find to join its staff and organize a great system of technical schools, and research colleges to train the next generation of directors and managers. We should make a new map of the world for the purposes of the Council, a map which would pay very little heed to the old out-of-date political divisions of the world. We should mark out copper districts and coal districts, corn lands and pasture lands, forest belts and cotton lands, instead of kingdoms and states. We should study the mountain ranges and watersheds with a view to water distribution and transport, we should try to keep people speaking the same language together because that would be more convenient, and, since mountains and seas and economic habits have always played a certain part in distributing humanity and determining its local characters, we might find when our map was drawn out that many of its lines would, after all, follow existing boundaries. Of course that new mapping for economic convenience is absolutely essential if we are really out to end war. By the end of my Dictatorship everything would be grown where it was most conveniently grown for production and distribution, and I should hope to have not a single custom house left in the world. Goods would be moving as easily and cheaply about our planet, from producer to consumer, as now they shift from one end of a big modern factory to another.

There would have to be one money in the world. That is a matter now of considerable urgency, and the first task almost of my Dictatorship (or yours) would be to see to that. It is manifest to everyone now that the existing cash and credit system is breaking down. It is ancient and worn out. It is rotten. The industrial life of the world is being strangled in an immense tangle of debts. Almost my first administrative act would be to state the plain fact of the case and declare the world bankrupt. That means—I am afraid that here I must cut some corners—that debts have to be written down. The only practical way in which a community or a world can make a settlement of excessive debts is to depreciate the currency in which they are reckoned. A bankrupt is bankrupt relatively to the rest of the community. He pays so much in the pound and we discharge him. But what we have to do with here is not a relative bankruptcy but a general bankruptcy. The people of the earth, the industries of the people of the earth, cannot pay their way. And for a whole community which cannot pay its way the only way of writing down its debts is to write down the currency by which those debts are reckoned. In other words, prices have to be put up. Production is being paralyzed by prices too low to yield a profit and pay rent, interest on loans, and wages, and producers are therefore unable to pay debts or consume. So we stagger through distress towards catastrophe.

But here we are confronted to-day by the difficulty that these affairs are not under one single control, but under a number of separate governments, with time-honoured, but now stupid and dangerous, traditions of competition and conflict. It is easy to say that currency should be depreciated and prices inflated, but very hard to carry that out in any but a futile, dangerous local way. The great states of the world have not even a common money by which to measure their relations, through which they could effect this necessary debt-relieving operation. And they are not all equally insolvent. Some are deeper in trouble than others, and at different phases of misfortune. Disaster is world-wide, but it has different aspects in different countries. Money means different things in different countries.

For nearly a hundred years before the War, because of the great gold production of Africa, Australia, California, and the Klondyke, the golden sovereign was practically a world coin. But now, for reasons too complex to examine in such a talk as this, the gold standard is failing us. A crazy competition for gold is in progress between the leading states of the world, credit staggers drunkenly, and great masses of humanity are falling into the direst need and distress, because of the fragmentary, incoherent way in which the world's book-keeping is done. In times of catastrophe vigorous measures are needed. At the outset of my Dictatorship I should restrict the issue of money to one central world authority; I should fix the exchange value of existing currencies to one another and to this new currency; I should gradually call in the old currencies altogether. And my central monetary authority would see to it that the ratios of the new world money to the old standards of reckoning secured just that inflation of prices and just that diminution of the burthen of debts needed to restore productive activity to the world. A single world currency and a world-controlled credit system, it seems to me, constitute a necessary preliminary to that rationalization of economic life which is the only sure foundation of world peace and prosperity.

Remember I am telling you what I should do were I World Dictator. So I sound rather dogmatic. But I do not expect you to accept this conclusion of mine. Only—if my answer is wrong, what is your answer? I have put before you the broad lines on which I believe the peace and prosperity of mankind can be established. Set my answer aside—that does not let you set my question aside.

There are other points in that question I have still to say a word about. Given peace on earth and abundance for all, will there not be a rapid and indeed a frightful increase of population and a great clash of races? Here again I must answer in a sentence or so. As World Dictator I should see to it that the kind of knowledge which leads to a restriction of population is spread throughout the whole world. That secured, I do not think mankind need fear over-population. Nor do I think the races of mankind are going to devour one another. There is not going to be any great overrunning of peoples. The climatic regions of the earth determine the character of their human populations. The negro did not capture tropical Africa; tropical Africa made him and gave herself to him; for keeps, I think. The brownish peoples again hold the subtropical world by virtue of their superior adaptation to that world; similarly the whites the rainy temperate zone, and the Mongols dry Asia. So it seems to me. There may be a lot of marginal admixture; there may be replacement with altered conditions: but *my* World Dictatorship at any rate will be untroubled by the nightmare of racial swarmings. Men in the coming future will find that when they are free to move wherever they choose about our planet they will for the most part stay in the habitats congenial to them. When they know how to limit their increases they will limit them. The great migrations of the past have been hunger marches, and my economic controls and my population controls will have put an end to such disturbances.

And how am I going to *fix* this new world rule of mine so that peace and prosperity will remain when the world is released from my Dictatorship? By an immense reorganization of education. Because, as I am sure you know, for all practical purposes education is nothing more nor less than fitting the natural man, his ideas and his will, to the social state in which he has to live. You cannot change education without presently producing corresponding changes in social life; you cannot make any real and permanent changes in human life unless you educate the young for it. I have always been a believer in education—the right sort of education—and my faith increases with the years. My Dictatorship will be essentially an Educational Dictatorship. Every great change in political, social, and economic life demands a corresponding educational change. For the better part of twenty years the schools and colleges of the world will march *forward*. For the better part of twenty years I shall have the young forgetting their old, narrow, bloodstained histories and learning of the great adventure of mankind—and not only the young; I should enormously extend adult education. By the time my Dictatorship is done the new economic life, the new and simpler money, the achievement of world unity, will be understood by nearly everybody in the world under forty, and by a large majority over that age. They will all know what they are doing. By the time when my retirement falls due the restoration of our present way of living would be almost as practicable as the restoration of the Heptarchy or the Stone Age.

But it may be objected to what I am saying that I am really proposing to push the existing sovereign militant governments of the world aside and providing no substitute. Well, what if I am? Do we want a world parliament or a world president, a world flag, or indeed anything of that sort? It seems to me that nothing in that form is required. A world control would be necessarily different from an existing government, because it would not be militant. A world control means a stupendous *simplification* of human affairs. There would be a world economic control board, a central police control which would arise naturally out of that peace and disarmament board I talked about at first, and a great world organization sustaining education, scientific research, and the perpetual revision of ideas. These boards would carry on (and they are really all that is needed for carrying on) the essential business of this planet. Why should there be a world parliament? It would have to meet in the tower of Babel—and what would there be for it to do? Would there be world elections? About what? Would there be great world politicians and leaders of the world people? Upon what issues?

But it may be asked, Who will make the ultimate decision? There must be a king or an assembly, or some such body, to say "Yes" or "No," in the last resort. But must there be? Suppose your intellectual organization, your body of thought, your scientific men, say and prove that this, that, or the other course is the *right* one. Suppose they have the common-sense of an alert and educated community to sustain them. Why should not a dictatorship—not of this man or that man, nor of the proletariat, but of informed and educated common-sense—some day rule the earth? What need is there for a lot of politicians and lawyers to argue about the way things ought to be done, confusing the issues? Why make a dispute of world welfare? What need is there for some autocrat to say "Yes" or "No" when a course is known to be sound and right? You do not let politicians and rulers run the engineering enterprises of mankind, you do not make public health a political question. Why should professional squabbles of that sort mess about with the world's economic life, or world education, or keeping the peace?

But let me be quite clear about existing governments, flags, and so forth. There is no need to *abolish* such things. I am no red-handed revolutionary, no destructive firebrand tearing down venerable things. All I should do, as World Dictator, would be to deprive these governments of the power and means of making war, relieve them of supreme financial and economic control, and take the general direction and protection of education and scientific research throughout the world out of their hands, by requiring them to be set up, or by setting up competent overriding bodies. They would no longer be sovereign powers to that extent, but that is not saying they are to be forcibly extinguished or robbed suddenly of the respect tradition accords them. If they are useful in their attenuated forms, they will survive; if they are useless, they will fade out harmlessly.

There, briefly, is my answer to my own question. That is what I would do with the world, and what I believe could be done with the world *now*. And in this way I think life might be made beyond comparison fuller and happier than it is. You may think my plan is bold or wild or Utopian or undesirable or impossible. But you would have thought it much wilder and more impossible a year or so ago, before you began to learn about the Russian Five Year Plan. A time may come when such a project as this will seem obvious to everyone. And whatever you think of my answer, I beg of you to consider my question—which poses in effect this riddle—"What are you and I and the others up to—if we are not merely drifting upon the stream of fate?"

Reject my answer. Reject this idea of federal world controls—controls of money and credit, controls of trade and education and scientific organization, controls to keep the peace. Then find another answer to the questions that confront us. The question I have put to you is only a device for getting the complex of human difficulties into a compact and answerable form, to simplify it down to a personal challenge to you.

What has to be done about war?

What has to be done about the world's faltering and failing economic life?

What of money and credit—which are plainly no longer working properly?

What of population and race?

What of education?

Those who have answers, those who even attempt answers to these questions, are playing a part in human destiny. But those who have no answer and make no attempt to get one are just human animals, to be chased about by events, luckily or unluckily, until they die.

Bibliography

Gascoigne, Bamber
    1993   *Encyclopedia of Britain.* New York: Macmillan.

Kenyon, J.P.
    1994   *The Wordsworth Dictionary of British History.* Ware, England: Wordsworth Reference.

Stover, Leon
    1987   *The Prophetic Soul: A Reading of H.G. Wells's "Things to Come."* Jefferson, N.C., and London: McFarland.
    1996–2003   *The Annotated H.G. Wells:* seven volumes [the present work is the eighth]. Jefferson, N.C.: McFarland. List of titles on the first page of the present volume

H.G. Wells

1896   *The Wheels of Chance: A Holiday Adventure.* London: J.M. Dent.
1898   "The Man Who Could Work Miracles." *Illustrated London News,* July. In 1927a.
1902   *Anticipations of the Reaction of Mechanical and Scientific Progress Upon Human Life and Thought.* New York: Harper & Brothers.
1905   *A Modern Utopia.* London: Chapman & Hall.
1905a   *Kipps: The Story of a Simple Soul.* London: Macmillan.
1906   *Socialism and the Family.* London: A.C. Field.
1906a   *In the Days of the Comet.* London: Macmillan.
1913   *The Passionate Friends.* New York: Harper & Brothers.
1914   *Social Forces in England and America.* New York: Harper & Brothers.
1914a   *The World Set Free.* London: Macmillan.
1914b   Introduction to *Anticipations* (1902), second edition. London: Chapman & Hall, pp. vii–xiii.
1915   *Boon, the Mind of the Race.* London: T. Fisher Unwin.
1915a   *The Peace of the World.* London: The Daily Chronicle.
1920   *The Outline of History.* London: Cassell.
1922   *Washington and the Hope of Peace.* London: Collins.
1923   *Men Like Gods.* New York: Macmillan.
1927   *Democracy Under Revision.* New York: George H. Doran.
1927a   *The Short Stories of H.G. Wells.* London: Ernest Benn.
1928   "Has the Money-Credit System a Mind? *The Banker* 6:221–233.

(H.G. Wells, *continued*)

1931   *The Work, Wealth, and Happiness of Mankind.* Two volumes. Garden City, N.Y.: Doubleday, Doran.
1931a   *What Are We to Do with Our Lives?* Garden City, N.Y.: Doubleday, Doran.
1932   *After Democracy: Forecasts of the World State.* London: Watts.
1933   *The Shape of Things to Come: The Ultimate Revolution.* London: Hutchinson.
1934   *Whither Mankind?* Film treatment of *Things to Come*, in Stover 1987, Appendix I, pages 121–179.
1934a   *Experiment in Autobiography.* New York: Macmillan.
1935   *Things to Come: A Film Story Based on the Material Contained in His History of the Future "The Shape of Things to Come."* London: Cresset.
1936   *Things to Come.* Release script of the London Films Production, in Stover 1987, Appendix II.
1944   *'42 to '44: A Contemporary Memoir Upon Human Behavior During the Crisis of the World Revolution.* London: Secker & Warburg.

Index

BBC 1, 130
Brahma 2, 4; *see also* Hindu trinity

Cleopatra 49*n*21
Colbert, Claudette 49*n*21
Copernicus 87*n*43

Darwin, Charles 111
DeMille, Cecil B. 49*n*21

Fotheringay Castle (Scotland) 4

Harding, President Warren G. 86*n*42
Hitler, Adolf 45*n*19, 69*n*34, 85*n*42
Hindu Trinity 1, 2, 3, 4, 66*n*30; *see also* Brahma; Siva; Vishnu

inertia, physics of 80*n*41

Jeans, Sir James 53*n*23
Joshua, Book of 32*n*12; 87*n*43

Korda, Alexander 1

Lenin, V.I. 45*n*19; Five Year Plan 130

Marx, Karl 24*n*8, 45*n*19, 60*n*27
Mary, Queen of Scots 4

Massey, Raymond 10*n*1
Mussolini, Benito 45*n*19, 85*n*42

Plato 2, 3, 91*n*45; *Republic* 4

Revelation, Book of 111, 117
Richardson, Ralph 10*n*1, 59*n*26

Shelley, Percy Bysshe 56*n*24
Siva 2, 4; *see also* Hindu trinity
Stalin, Joseph 10*n*1, 45*n*19, 130

Vishnu 2, 3, 4, 30*n*11, 38*n*15, 66*n*30, 67*n*32, 73*n*37; *see also* Hindu trinity

Washington Conference of 1921 86*n*42
Wells, H.G.: *After Democracy: Forecasts of the World State* 4, 130; *Anticipations* 66*n*31; *The Banker:* "Has the Money-Credit System a Mind?" 46*n*20; *Democracy Under Revision* 4; "The Human Adventure" 2; *In the Days of the Comet* 56*n*24; *The Invisible Man* 43*n*17; *Kipps: The Story of a Simple Soul* 24*n*8; "The Man Who Could Work Miracles" 10*n*1, 52, 95–110; *Men Like Gods* 15*n*2; *A Modern Utopia* 15*n*2, 24*n*8; *The Outline of History* 2; *The Peace of the World* 85*n*42; *The Shape of Things to Come* 10*n*1; *Socialism and the Family* 4; *Things to Come* (film) 1, 2, 3, 4, 10*n*1,

17n4, 57n25, 59n26, 66n30, 69n34, 80n41, 85n42, 91n45, 93n46, 117, 130; "Under the Knife" 117–129; "War with Tradition" 80n41; *Washington and the Hope of Peace*: "The Immensity of the Issue and the Triviality of Men" 86n42; "What I Would Do with the World" (radio broadcast) 130; *The Wheels of Chance* 24n8, 25; *The Work, Wealth, and Happiness of Mankind* 44n19; *The World Set Free* 3

World War I 85n42

Young, Roland 10n1